The Theories, Concepts and Practices of Democracy

Series Editors
Jean-Paul Gagnon, University of Canberra, Canberra, Australia
Mark Chou, Australian Catholic University, Fitzroy, Australia

There are many types of democracies and many types of democrats. Though contemporary Western scholars and practitioners of democracy have tended to repeat a particular set of narratives and discourses, recent research shows us that there are in fact hundreds of different adjectives of democracy. What one theorist, political leader or nation invokes as democracy, others may label as something altogether different. Part of this has to do with the political nature of democracy. As a practice and concept, it is always contested. Yet instead of exploring these differences and ambiguities, many democrats today retreat to the well-worn definitions and practices made popular by Western powers in the twentieth-century.

The aim of this book series is to engage and explore democracy's many articulations. It seeks contributions which critically define, analyse and organise the many theories, concepts and practices that encompass democracy in all its forms. Both theoretical and empirical treatments of democracy, particularly when told from less conventional or more marginal perspectives, are especially encouraged.

Rico Isaacs

Political Opposition in Authoritarianism

Exit, Voice and Loyalty in Kazakhstan

Rico Isaacs
University of Lincoln
Lincoln, UK

ISSN 2947-4469   ISSN 2947-4477   (electronic)
The Theories, Concepts and Practices of Democracy
ISBN 978-3-031-06535-4   ISBN 978-3-031-06536-1   (eBook)
https://doi.org/10.1007/978-3-031-06536-1

© The Author(s), under exclusive license to Springer Nature Switzerland AG 2022

This work is subject to copyright. All rights are solely and exclusively licensed by the Publisher, whether the whole or part of the material is concerned, specifically the rights of translation, reprinting, reuse of illustrations, recitation, broadcasting, reproduction on microfilms or in any other physical way, and transmission or information storage and retrieval, electronic adaptation, computer software, or by similar or dissimilar methodology now known or hereafter developed.

The use of general descriptive names, registered names, trademarks, service marks, etc. in this publication does not imply, even in the absence of a specific statement, that such names are exempt from the relevant protective laws and regulations and therefore free for general use.

The publisher, the authors, and the editors are safe to assume that the advice and information in this book are believed to be true and accurate at the date of publication. Neither the publisher nor the authors or the editors give a warranty, expressed or implied, with respect to the material contained herein or for any errors or omissions that may have been made. The publisher remains neutral with regard to jurisdictional claims in published maps and institutional affiliations.

Cover illustration: © John Rawsterne/patternhead.com

This Palgrave Macmillan imprint is published by the registered company Springer Nature Switzerland AG
The registered company address is: Gewerbestrasse 11, 6330 Cham, Switzerland

For Liga

Acknowledgements

This work is the product of 17 years of thinking, writing and talking about opposition politics in authoritarian regimes and specifically in Kazakhstan. Elements of this research were written up in various forms before I finally settled on a longer form essay as the optimum format which could do justice to the ideas and findings of the Kazakhstani case of opposition agency. Consequently, I am indebted to several colleagues who have commented only on earlier iterations of this work and who provided crucial feedback as I worked through the ideas in this book including Gary Browning, Togzhan Kassenova, Liga Rudzite, Regine Spector, Sarah Whitmore and especially Neil Robinson who inspired my interest in Albert Hirschman's work. Over the last seven years I have presented numerous versions of this essay to audiences including at Oxford Brookes University, the University of Limerick, New College Oxford and the Association of Nationalism Studies convention at Colombia University. On each occasion the discussion and questions from the audience were invaluable in shaping my thoughts on opposition politics in authoritarian regimes. As ever, mistakes in this work remain my sole responsibility.

The data used in this essay was collected across a period from 2006 to 2019 with field trips to Kazakhstan made possible through several grant awards. This includes a Leverhulme Trust Fellowship (RF-2018-188\8), a British Academy Small Grant (SG101607) and a Leverhulme Study Abroad Studentship (SAS/30161), I am grateful to these awarding bodies for enabling the fieldwork to take place through their financial support.

During fieldwork which took place in 2006–2007, 2011–2012, 2014 and 2019 I was aided by exemplary research assistants who helped with the organisation and conduct of interviews. Many thanks go to Kerim Nuriyev, Mariya Kuliyeva, Aidana Abdykulova, Nikolay Shevchenko and Gulzhanat Gafu for all their help and assistance over these years.

I am grateful to the team at Palgrave, especially Ambra Finotello, for giving the go ahead to this publication and Ashwini Elango for keeping the publication on track. Finally, I am especially thankful for the resilience and resolve of Liga. The last 2 years have been traumatic and challenging, but we persevere together in strength and love and that makes every day easy.

Contents

1 Introduction: Authoritarian Institutions, Regimes and Political Opposition ... 1

Part I Opposition Agency and Opposition-Regime Relations in Authoritarianism

2 Defining, Conceptualising and Theorising Opposition-Regime Relations in Authoritarian Regimes ... 21

3 Exit, Voice and Loyalty: An Analytical Framework for Opposition Agency in Authoritarian Regimes ... 41

Part II Exit, Voice and Loyalty in Kazakhstan

4 The Development of a Personalist-Authoritarianism Regime in Kazakhstan ... 57

5 Exit, Voice and Loyalty—Opposition Strategies and Choice from Above in Kazakhstan, 1998–2011 ... 75

6 Non-oligarchic Public Voice in Kazakhstan from Below, 2011–2022 ... 97

7 Conclusion ... 127

Glossary ... 135

Bibliography 137

Index 157

List of Figures

Fig. 3.1　Four nodal point political opposition agency matrix in authoritarian systems　49

Fig. 3.2　Mutually constitutive cycle of regime and opposition in authoritarian settings　52

LIST OF TABLES

Table 3.1   Types of sanctions   48
Table 5.1   Signatures to the creation of DVK, 18 November 2001   82

CHAPTER 1

Introduction: Authoritarian Institutions, Regimes and Political Opposition

THE 'INSTITUTIONAL TURN' AS AN ENTRY POINT TO OPPOSITION

Studies of comparative authoritarianism have become increasingly complex and sophisticated in the last two decades. Scholars have sought to comprehend not just what leads to the momentous upheaval from autocracy to democracy, but rather the resilience of authoritarian regimes over time (Dimitrov, 2013, 1). The classical literature on authoritarianism, typically framed the control and durability of non-democratic regimes through the lens of coercion. As Hannah Arendt understood, terror had been used to exterminate and frighten opponents, but in the totalitarian regimes of the twentieth century, terror became a coercive instrument to rule masses of people (Arendt, 1951, 6). In this way, totalitarian regimes, the harshest model of non-democratic rule, were perceived to largely base attempts at durability via the encompassing terror and propaganda fed into the daily lives of citizens (Friedrich & Brzezinski, 1956). But coercion alone is never enough for sustained non-democratic rule. Analysis of bureaucratic authoritarian regimes, like those observed in the 1960s and 1970s in Latin America, illustrated how such regimes which combined both military rule and technocratism sought durability based on the development and rationalisation of the economy (O'Donnell, 1988). At the same time, corporatist authoritarian regimes in the same continent were able to suspend challenge to their rule through a system of interest representation in which specific agencies were given representational monopoly over their field in exchange for observing certain controls on their selection of leaders and articulation of demands and supports (Schmitter, 1974, 93–94).

Implicitly, corporatism tends to underlie much of the contemporary scholarship on understanding authoritarian resilience. The 'institutional turn' in comparative authoritarianism illustrated the importance of political institutions in providing authoritarian elites with mechanisms for the co-optation and incorporation of opposition and potential rivals (Brownlee, 2007; Gandhi, 2008; Geddes, 2006; Magaloni & Kricheli, 2010; Pepinsky, 2014). As Svolik (2012) has noted, authoritarian rule is concerned with the dilemmas of authoritarian control and power-sharing. Parties and legislatures are theorised to play a role in assisting the distribution of economic transfers and rents to co-opt potential rivals (Magaloni & Kricheli, 2010, 126) and by offering policy concessions (Gandhi & Przeworski, 2006; Lust-Okar, 2005; Magaloni & Kricheli, 2010; Reuter & Robertson, 2015). In more recent research, the process of policy concessions through legislatures has shown the way in which actors within the regime have divergent preferences and interests (Noble, 2020; Williamson & Magaloni, 2020), not too far from pluralist and corporatist accounts of political management in post-Stalinist USSR (Hough, 1983). Thus, co-optation and elite bargaining through institutions provide 'widely accepted mechanisms for resolving intraparty disputes and managing leadership succession' and thus help ward off threats to the regime aiding its durability and reproduction over time (Pepinsky, 2014, 633). The 'institutional turn' in comparative authoritarianism while overturning previously held assumptions that formal institutions tended to play a subversive role in authoritarian rule, as they did in the case of the former Yugoslavia and the Soviet Union (Bunce, 1999), also reflected 'real world' developments of the 'global tide of authoritarianism' witnessed in the last two decades (Glasius, 2018, 515).

Thus, the emergence of scholarship which has focused on the role of political institutions points to the greater complexity of authoritarianism. Ultimately, this is not a book about political institutions in authoritarianism, but it does take the 'institutional turn' as a starting point to speak to a different facet of authoritarian rule, one which on outward appearances does not lack for points of reference in the scholarship on authoritarianism, but one in which underneath the surface our understanding remains constrained: political opposition. The dilemmas faced by authoritarian regimes of political control and power sharing, as noted by Svolik (2012), all hinge on the leadership's ability and capacity to solve these dilemmas in relation to political opposition. The game of co-optation and policy concessions between regime and opposition is usually predicated on the regime making the first move and the opposition responding accordingly. As such, studies of opposition in authoritarian contexts have characteristically focused on the regime's ability to counter opposition elites and movements and their activities using co-optation or policy concessions to bargain with opposition elites (Gandhi & Przeworski, 2006; Magaloni & Kricheli, 2010; La Porte, 2014; Lust-Okar, 2005) or to use practices of electoral manipulation or 'tool kits' to marginalise and stifle opposition (Kevlihan & Ó Beacháin, 2017; Schedler, 2002, 2006; Schatz, 2009).

But how can we understand this relationship between regime and opposition? In the authoritarian context the relationship between regime and opposition tends to be characterised as an equilibrium that often manifests itself in two ways. The first concerns the relationship between dissent and repression and the extent to which a rise in one can precipitate a rise in the other. Repression sparks dissent and dissent sparks repression. Opposition and regime then get locked into a spiralling cycle until a tipping point is reached and either the opposition is distinguished completely, or resentment of the regime is mobilised into a full-scale uprising. The second, is the way in which regime and opposition get locked into a co-dependent relationship via co-optation. As we have seen from scholarship in the 'institutional turn', non-democratic rulers can offer jobs, resources and other spoils in exchange for support and loyalty from opposition elites. Consequently, each side ends up depending on one another, the regime on the opposition for survival and the opposition on the regime for private goods.

These equilibria, in each instance, tend to focus on the agency[1] of the regime.[2] The opposition tends to be treated as the object rather than

---

[1] While recognising that agency is a contested concept, here it is understood as the ability of an individual, institution, or organisation, to act with a degree of freedom and without constraint to reproduce or shape wider social processes and structures (Giddens, 1994).

[2] These equilibria will be discussed more fully in this chapter.

subject and opposition agency tends to be under theorised and/or not drawn out specifically in the analysis. It is true of course, that agency was one of the configuring schools of thought of the transitology debate from the 1970s to the 1990s (O'Donnell & Schmitter, 1986; Rustow, 1970). But the interest then was on transition and the choices of both regime and opposition elites to enter a 'pact' to push forward political and economic reform, rather than on the agency available to opposition in recalcitrant regimes. At the same time, the regime-opposition equilibrium which enables autocratic regimes to broaden their base of support to stabilise and prolong their rule is understood to only succeed if opposition agency represents a *credible* threat to the regime (Boix & Svolik, 2013). Thus, there is an assumption that there is a clear binary understanding on the regime's part as to what constitutes credible or non-credible opposition. But this leaves open questions about instances where the threat from the opposition is more ambiguous. How does a regime respond to a case where it is difficult to ascertain whether the threat from the opposition is credible? What is the balance that regimes adopt in terms of co-optation versus coercive practices to stymie opposition challenges? And how might this effect or alter our understanding of equilibria which exist between regime and opposition in authoritarian systems? These are the two central themes of this book: to understand more fully the logic, dynamics and agency of opposition in an authoritarian setting and its impact on authoritarian resilience; and to complicate our understanding further by exploring the issue of opposition ambiguity—the grey zone between a credible and non-credible opposition.

WHY OPPOSITION?

Opposition may seem an anathema to authoritarianism. An authoritarian regime typically claims to rule in the interest of all sections of society, and those it does not claim to represent are often cast as the unrepresentable 'other'. This makes the idea that there should be any form of constitutionally designated opposition, or other forms of officially sanctioned challenge to authoritarian rulers, problematic. In an authoritarian regime, 'the integrity of the state and the responsibility of government' is symbolised usually in a single person or ruling clique and as Rodney Barker notes, 'it is difficult in practice to challenge one without the other' (Barker, 1971, 8) and this can explain why our understanding of the logic of opposition in authoritarian regimes remains largely limited and undeveloped as the central agent of change in an authoritarian system remains the regime.

The lack of emphasis on political opposition in authoritarian systems is entirely natural. With power concentrated in a single individual or small group of elites it is always the agency of the regime where attention will be drawn, even when a study is focused on opposition, as it is the regime which often possesses the agency to curtail and sanction challenges to its position. However, as with Robert Dahl's belief over 50 years ago that we need to examine opposition to understand modern democracy, so it is that we need to understand the logic of opposition to understand modern authoritarianism (Dahl, 1966, xviii). All political systems to some extent contain the expression and organisation of varied political preferences—even in totalitarian systems—it is part of our human condition to accumulate political preferences and seek to express them. As Dahl noted, 'during any given period, therefore, a political system will contain some people who, if there were no barriers or costs to their doing so, would oppose to the conduct of the government' (Dahl, 1971, 2). Thus, even if we do not see opposition agency as a primary phenomenon in authoritarian systems, it remains an important and integral human dynamic of such systems. Accordingly, we do need to conceptualise and explore the role of political opposition in authoritarian contexts, if only to understand greater the internal dynamics of authoritarian systems, and at the most it could offer the potential to understand regime and social change (Ionescu & de Madariaga, 1968, 2).

The importance of political opposition in authoritarianism, therefore, is that it is the counterpart to power and that together regime and opposition exist in a mutually constitutive relationship. The opposition is ultimately conditioned by the regime, impacted by their ability to participate in the political process and the extent to which they might gain access to spoils (Albrecht, 2015). At the same time, authoritarian regimes rely on the existence of opposition to manage threats to its stability, which it can eliminate via co-optation, concessions and/or repression. In this way, opposition can act as a feedback signal, alerting the regime to deficiencies and gaps in its power. Therefore, a focus on opposition agency is important for understanding exactly how authoritarian regimes can be either durable or fallible in the longer term.

As already alluded to, this mutually constitutive relationship is often conceived as an equilibrium. But the existing scholarship underplays opposition agency and over focuses on the regime within these conceptualisations of equilibria, emphasising the power and logic of the regime in shaping authoritarian resilience and opposition prospects. This book seeks instead to explore how opposition agency shapes regime outcomes, particularly in a context where the credibility of the opposition is ambiguous. One case where we can observe a mutually constitutive relationship between opposition and regime, where opposition agency shapes regime outcomes and where the opposition is viewed ambiguously by the regime as both credible and non-credible, is Kazakhstan.

Why Kazakhstan?

Kazakhstan is an ideal example of a contemporary authoritarian state within which to locate a study of opposition-regime relations. For the nearly 30 years he was in power, the first president of Kazakhstan, Nursultan Nazarbayev, built a highly centralised political executive which suffocated alternative sites of power, and in the process constructed a highly personalised patronal regime (Hale, 2014) in which power was built upon the patronage and distribution of spoils given out by Nazarbayev and his closest political associates (Isaacs, 2011).

If we want to understand opposition agency, opposition-regime relations and their impact on regime stability, then a country in which authoritarianism has been well-built but yet at the same time also rocked by internal shocks to regime stability (e.g., 2001 with the emergence of *Demokraticheskii Vybor Kazakhstana* (Democratic Choice of Kazakhstan [DVK]), the Zhanaozen protests of 2011, the land protests of 2016 and the 2019 protests against the regime in favour of fair elections, and the 2022 *Qandy Qantar* [bloody January]), then Kazakhstan is an aptly suited example.

At the same time, Kazakhstan presents a puzzling case. Kazakhstan is an authoritarian state[3] and from 1998 onwards the political system developed a political opposition which could be characterised as 'oligarchic': leading businessmen who accrued significant business portfolios during

---

[3] This article adopts a Linzian understanding of authoritarianism as 'political systems with limited […] political pluralism, without elaborate and guiding ideology, but with distinctive mentalities, without extensive mobilisation […] and in which a leader […] exercises power within formally ill-defined limits but actually quite predictable ones' (Linz, 2000, 79).

the privatisation of the Kazakhstani economy in the 1990s and who sought to turn these business interests into political influence (La Porte, 2017). A failure to successfully co-opt these elites through bargaining and rewards led to their fragmentation from the ruling elite into open public opposition. The literature within the 'institutional turn' would tell us that if these opposition elites were a credible threat, then the regime would have done everything in their power to co-opt them, which did not happen. But if they were not a credible threat the regime would not have gone to the significant lengths that it did from 1998 onwards to alter the institutional architecture to protect itself from threats to its stability from this political opposition.

An investigation into regime-opposition relations and opposition agency in Kazakhstan and its impact on policy and regime durability is well-positioned to reveal broader theoretical insights within the literature of comparative authoritarianism, not least when it comes to the 'institutional turn' and opposition-regime relations in general. The case of opposition agency and opposition-regime relations in Kazakhstan leaves us with a series of questions. How does Kazakhstani opposition agency contribute to the regime-opposition equilibrium in this instance, especially in terms of the opposition's ambiguously perceived credibility? How might opposition agency shape regime outcomes and the dynamics of opposition over time in an authoritarian state? And how might opposition agency contribute to regime stability over time?

This book tackles these questions through an analysis of Kazakhstani opposition agency and its relationship with the regime over a period of 20 years, drawing on a wealth of interview data from 14 years of research in-field in Kazakhstan speaking with opposition elites, activists, regime elites, journalists, local experts and NGO activists along with many informal conversations with ordinary citizens.[4] Through a thematic analysis of data, triangulated with documentary data such as print and online media sources, first-hand accounts of political opposition experience, legislation and policy reports, among others, a series of granular

---

[4] This includes 90 semi-structured interviews from 2006 to 2019 over numerous fieldtrips which took place in 2006–2007, 2011–2012, 2014, 2016 and 2019. These interviews formed parts of different research projects examining the role of political parties in Kazakhstan, the process of election observation, art and politics in Kazakhstan, opposition politics and youth and political opposition. This essay does not draw on all interviews undertaken but is informed by them all and the broader observations accumulated from 14 years studying and working infield in Kazakhstan.

categories were established in relation to opposition in Kazakhstan and the nature of opposition agency in the country. These categories were then abstracted upwards in a dialectical manner to establish the broader conceptual frames pertaining to disaggregating and defining opposition in authoritarian regimes and in conceptualising opposition agency and its relationship to the regime through the frame of exit, voice and loyalty.

Exit, Voice and Loyalty—Opposition Agency

At the root of this study is an appeal to prioritise our understanding of opposition agency in authoritarian contexts. This requires introducing a framework to help us understand not just the nature of opposition agency, the strategies and choices available to political opposition in Kazakhstan, but also how such agency can shape regime outcomes. I adopt Albert Hirschman's conceptual framework of exit, voice and loyalty to undertake such a task. The categories of exit, voice and loyalty were conceived by Hirschman to explore the options for customers in the face of the deterioration of a firm's output. Hirschman argued that there were two possible responses to decline in product quality. Consumers could stop buying the product and 'exit' the organisation or alternatively they could 'express their dissatisfaction directly to the management', in other words empower their 'voice' to enforce change (Hirschman, 1970). Loyalty was also introduced to explain why some consumers persist with voice despite a decline in the organisation.

Hirschman's framework has been applied to a range of contexts, including various political situations, not least Hirschman himself who used it to analyse the extent to which exit enabled or undermined voice in the German Democratic Republic and how this contributed to the collapse of the East German state (Hirschman, 1993). Similarly, others have focused on the role of migration as a form of exit (Dalmasso, 2018; Hoffmann, 2010; Landgrave & Nowrasteh, 2016; Moses, 2005; Pfaff & Kim, 2003; Sippola, 2013). Exit, voice and loyalty has been used to frame other aspects of politics too, including attitudes of ethnic Russians in post-Soviet Estonia (Evans, 1998), political participation in pre-industrial societies (Ross, 1988), communication strategies of Swiss and Italian populists (Albertazzi, 2009), voter trust in Belgian regional elections (Hooge et al., 2011) and in relation to public administration and public choice theory (Witt, 2011).

This is not an exhaustive list of where exit, voice, loyalty has been used in political studies nor, of course the multitude of disciplines within which the frame has been adopted such as organisational studies, psychology, sociology and this list could go on. Hirschman's framework has become ubiquitous and for good reason. It has an elegant and simple equation at its heart which speaks to the capacity, or absence of capacity, of human agency. Exit, voice and loyalty is appealing for the way in which we can understand simple agential choices that confront us in every day and extraordinary situations. It is, therefore, a universal conceptualisation of human agency, easily understandable and entirely relatable.

Naturally, this study of opposition politics in Kazakhstan and opposition-regime relations builds upon this existing political studies scholarship which has adopted the exit, voice, loyalty as a frame. As will be elaborated at greater length in Chapter 2, the case of opposition agency via exit, voice and loyalty in Kazakhstan helps us complicate the exit-voice frame and does so in two ways. Firstly, by initially focusing on elite opposition agency this book challenges existing studies which demonstrate how elite opposition exit and voice serves to strengthen authoritarian institutions (Langston, 2002). While ostensibly the case of elite exit and voice in Kazakhstan does assist in bolstering the authoritarian regime, as opposition agency provides a feedback signal to which the regime reacts with sanctions and institutional adaptation, over time the signal weakens because of the foreclosing of elite opposition leaving the regime unprepared for spontaneous non-elite grassroots-based opposition. Secondly, the case of Kazakhstan illustrates that opposition agency through exit and voice is not a straightforward binary choice. Opposition agency can entail both exit and voice simultaneously and moreover, there are different forms of voice and exit. This study of Kazakhstan will illustrate the complex, multifaceted and dynamic nature of exit, voice and loyalty which is often context dependent. The second part of the book will detail empirically how opposition agency in Kazakhstan illustrates that there are different forms of exit and various types of voice and there are multiple combinations between them. Exit and voice is not the straightforward dichotomy it is often assumed or presented as being.

Argument and Structure of the Work

This book offers a study of opposition agency in Kazakhstan, using Hirschman's exit, voice, loyalty framework to understand the agency of political opposition in the country and its impact on regime-opposition relations and regime resilience. The study finds that opposition agency in Kazakhstan can be understood as a series of choices between exit, voice and loyalty, but this appears in a multitude of ways: elite voice inside the regime; elite exit from the regime (with or without voice); non-elite voice outside the regime; exit from the country/political system (with or without voice). These variations can act as an important feedback signal for the regime, illustrating deficiencies in both dilemmas of power sharing and control, but also with broader public policy preferences. In responding to these feedback signals the regime reacts by applying a combination of sanctions (coercion) and/or institutional adaptation (but rarely policy concessions or power sharing) to shore up its position. However, the Nazarbayev regime's ambiguous treatment of opposition as neither credible nor non-credible meant it relied too heavily on sanctions and institutional adaptation which restricted and marginalised political opposition. Consequently, this served to limit the feedback signals exit and voice provided which in turn created greater social discontent in the shape of spontaneous grassroots opposition. The resulting impact placed the regime at risk because of the lack of formal institutional space for the airing of grievances (typically material and ideational). From 2011 onwards this is what occurred in Kazakhstan as a series of 'shocks' appeared from the ground up which shook the stability of the regime. This included the 2011 Zhanaozen oil workers protest, the 2016 land protests, the 2019 election protests and the protests and violence of January 2022.

What the case of Kazakhstan reveals to us in terms of the broader comparative politics of opposition-regime relations in authoritarian systems is that focusing on regime agency via strategies of exit, voice or loyalty allows us to understand the specific ways in which opposition agency can shape regime responses through sanctions and institutional adaptation which might increase regime stability in the short term, but only serve to establish greater regime instability over the long term. In the case of Kazakhstan, in treating the oligarchic opposition ambiguously, by viewing it as neither a credible nor non-credible threat, the regime served to disrupt the regime-opposition equilibrium. This then created the foundations for social upheaval in which the authorities were unable to manage, address and contain the different protests and claims against it by spontaneous non-oligarchic grassroots opposition. By failing to see opposition threats as wholly credible, the Nazarbayev regime over relied on coercive practices such as sanctions and institutional adaptation. While such acts insulated the regime from the initial oligarchic opposition threat, it failed ultimately to produce regime stability.

This book is divided into two main sections. The first provides a conceptual and theoretical grounding for understanding opposition-regime relations in non-democratic settings and is divided into two chapters. The first chapter discusses how we can best understand and define opposition in authoritarian contexts and specifically in the former Soviet space. The analysis claims that opposition in authoritarian regimes in the Eurasian space is typically understood in institutional and organisational terms, essentially in the form of political parties. Instead, I make the case that we need to move beyond an institutional formulation to adopt a wider definition of opposition in non-democratic regimes that includes individual forms of opposition (high-ranking individuals, nominally oligarchs), organisational (political parties and public movements) and 'spontaneous' grass roots-based opposition. Moreover, it argues that in the case of Kazakhstan, and to some extent the broader post-Soviet space, there is a particular 'oligarchic' quality to opposition which needs to be taken account. The chapter then goes onto elaborate on the two principal ways scholars of comparative authoritarianism have theorised opposition-regime equilibria: that between dissent and repression; and the other through a co-dependent relationship of co-optation. In the latter, authoritarian rulers view the opposition as a credible threat and offer jobs, resources and other spoils in exchange for support. Either side ends up depending on one another. What this chapter then argues is that existing theoretical models of regime-opposition relations do not take close enough account of opposition agency nor how a regime might adopt an ambiguous approach to opposition credibility. The question this leaves is: how can we best conceptualise opposition agency and relations in the Kazakh case to draw out its theoretical and conceptual contribution to our wider understanding of comparative authoritarianism?

The second chapter in the first section sets out to answer the above question by setting out a two-part analytical framework. The first part utilises Albert Hirschman's concept of exit, voice and loyalty to study oligarchic opposition agency in authoritarian regimes. The framework consists of four different variations of exit and/or voice: elite voice inside the regime; elite exit from the regime (with or without voice); non-elite voice outside the regime; and exit from the country/political system (with or without voice). The second part of the framework conceptualises regime-opposition relations as a form of equilibrium in which opposition agency of one of the variations of exit and/or voice is countered by the regime by either sanctions or institutional adaptation. Either response serves to marginalise the opposition and weaken the feedback signal opposition agency provides regarding discontent towards the regime. Without the feedback signal the regime is unprepared for future opposition agency of either exit or voice making it vulnerable to protest and regime instability.

The second section is divided into three chapters. The first provides an overview of the development of personalist authoritarianism in Kazakhstan. It briefly traces the Soviet origins of contemporary authoritarianism in Kazakhstan, before analysing the emergence of early forms of Soviet and post-Soviet political opposition, and the gradual foreclosing of parliamentary and institutional forms of political opposition in the 1990s. With the gradual marginalisation of institutional opposition, the Nazarbayev regime constructed a highly personalised form of authoritarian rule where legitimation became centred on the personal attributes of the leader built upon a patronal form of politics in which resources and spoils were distributed to competing elite groups. In such a context, formal constitutional changes were used to restrict and close the public sphere. Early post-Soviet forms of opposition were crushed and freedoms of assembly and speech, along with an independent media, were tightly controlled. The only place for political opposition to emerge in this context was from inside the regime itself in the shape of an oligarchic opposition, closely tied to key business and political elites.

The second chapter in this section takes three of the four different types of exit, voice and loyalty spelled out previously in chapter two and provides an account of how oligarchic opposition in Kazakhstan moved through the different nodal points of exit and voice, while the regime responded with sanctions and institutional adaptation. The chapter begins by analysing three examples of voice inside the regime by oligarchic opposition. The Nazarbayev regime failed to see this opposition as a credible threat and did not offer co-optation in exchange for support. Instead, these oligarchic opposition elites moved to the second nodal point and exited the regime while using public voice against Nazarbayev and the political system he established. This led to a response on behalf of the regime which included personal sanctions against the individuals involved in the opposition including tax fraud investigations, arrests, prosecution and harassment and institutional adaptation featuring changes to the law on political parties, law on elections and the constitution which sought to marginalise and penalise the oligarchic opposition. The paradox being that the regime saw the threat of opposition post-1998 as a credible enough threat to go to great lengths to marginalise and push them out of the political process. The tough regime response in terms of sanctions and institutional adaptation led to the third nodal point which was the exit of opposition from the political system itself and in some instances the country. The chapter details the experiences of leading figures from Kazakhstan's 'oligarchic' opposition who either left the political system and remained silent given the toll individual sanctions had taken on their careers and lives, or the country, where they continued to use voice against the regime. What the chapter argues is that while in the short term this insulated the regime from further threats to its stability, it closed off the feedback signal opposition agency, via exit and voice, provided. Once this feedback signal had been removed by the early 2010s the regime was left vulnerable to unpredictable voice from outside the oligarchic opposition.

The final chapter in this section focuses on the agency of non-oligarchic opposition 'from below' which emerged with the gradual decline of Kazakhstan's oligarchic opposition. Unable to grasp the preferences and interests of sections of the population, a series of 'shocks' from below rocked the stability of the Nazarbayev regime, all of which were unsuspecting and ultimately spontaneous (in that there was limited leadership or organisation 'from above'). This includes the six-month strike by oil workers in Zhanaozen in the West of the country in 2011; the large-scale protests which took place in 2016 regarding proposals the government had put forward concerning land reform; the protests which spread in the aftermath of Nazarbayev's resignation as president in 2019 which demanded free, honest and fair elections for his successor; and finally, the events of *qandy qantar* (bloody January) in 2022 which led to the end of the Nazarbayev era in Kazakhstan. The chapter explores these examples of spontaneous grassroots voice from below, how in each instance they took the regime by surprise and influenced and shaped regime policy regarding political reform. What the chapter highlights is how by foreclosing the oligarchic opposition it had closed off future feedback signals which could alert the regime to broader public concerns and regime deficiencies. While spontaneous grassroots opposition voice appeared as a series of 'shocks' to the regime, at the same time the regime floundered in its response, often unclear precisely as to whom to target sanctions at in response. Grassroots opposition voice was much harder to control and put back in the box once released, establishing ever increasing regime instability. The consequence of the 2022 *qandy qantar* events was a partial turnover of the regime through a process of de-Nazarbification. What the analysis highlights is how opposition agency through exit and voice can shape overall regime outcomes.

The concluding chapter of this work highlights four broad areas where the case of Kazakhstan contributes to our understanding of opposition agency in authoritarian systems. The first is that for a more fundamental understanding of the logic of opposition in authoritarian systems we need to broaden our conceptualisation of opposition actors beyond institutional forms such as political parties. The emergence of grassroots spontaneous opposition in Kazakhstan illustrates how non-institutional opposition can emerge as a powerful force, partly because of the closing down of institutional oppositional voice, which can then shape opposition-regime relations and ultimately broader systemic outcomes. Secondly, the analysis of Kazakhstan's opposition agency via exit and voice demonstrates, contrary to the existing literature, how the threat from political opposition can be ambiguously perceived by an authoritarian regime. The impact of this ambiguity, as the Kazakhstani case illustrates, is that the regime can act in an erratic way which on the surface seems strategically aimed at strengthening its position against perceived threats but cuts off future feedback signals which then undermines its stability because it is unaware of potential dissatisfaction from below. Thirdly, the case of Kazakhstani political opposition complicates the simple dichotomy between exit and voice in authoritarian systems. The analysis of opposition illustrates how the relationship between exit and voice is not a simple binary choice and nor a linear process. In the case of Kazakhstani political opposition there are at least four nodal points in terms of the choices between exit and voice. The essay demonstrates how exit and voice appear in numerous forms and combinations and importantly the agency of these different permutations of exit and voice are conditioned by the additional variables of sanctions and institutional adaptation. Finally, the case of Kazakhstan illustrates how authoritarian regimes which treat opposition threats ambiguously (rather than taking opposition seriously and seeking co-optation) are likely to end up in a continuous state of instability because the feedback provided by opposition agency disappears leaving the regime susceptible to grassroots, spontaneous opposition. It illustrates how opposition agency can be an important element of authoritarian regime durability, but also how authoritarian regimes can often end up in a paradoxical state of being simultaneously stable and unstable.

REFERENCES

Albertazzi, D. (2009). Reconciling 'voice' and 'exit': Swiss and Italian populists in power. *Politics, 29*(1), 1–10.

Albrecht, H. (2015). How can opposition support authoritarianism? Lessons from Egypt. *Democratization, 12*(30), 378–397.

Arendt, H. (1951). *The origins of totalitarianism*. Harcourt Press.

Barker, R. (1971). Introduction. In R. Barker (Ed.), *Studies in opposition* (pp. 1–30). Palgrave Macmillan.

Boix, C., & Svolik, M. (2013). The foundations of limited authoritarian government: Institutions, commitment, and power-sharing in dictatorships. *The Journal of Politics, 75*(2), 300–316.

Brownlee, J. (2007). *Authoritarianism in the age of democratisation*. Cambridge University Press.

Bunce, V. (1999). *Subversive institutions: The design and the collapse of socialism and the state*. Cambridge University Press.

Dahl, R. A. (Ed.). (1966). *Political oppositions in Western democracies*. Yale University Press.

Dahl, R. A. (1971). *Polyarchies: Participation and opposition*. Yale University Press.

Dalmasso, E. (2018). Participation without representation: Moroccans abroad at a time of unstable authoritarian rule. *Globalizations, 15*(2), 198–214.

Dimitrov, M. (2013). *Why communism did not collapse: Understanding authoritarian regime resilience in Asia and Europe*. Cambridge University Press.

Evans, G. (1998). Ethnic schism and the consolidation of post-communist democracies. *Communist and Post-Communist Studies, 31*(1), 57–74.

Friedrich, C., & Brzeinksi, Z. (1956). *Totalitarian dictatorship and autocracy*. Praeger.

Gandhi, J. (2008). *Political institutions under dictatorship*. Cambridge University. Press.

Gandhi, J., & Przeworski, A. (2006). Cooperation, co-optation, and rebellion under dictatorships. *Economics & Politics, 18*(1), 1–26.

Geddes, B. (2006). *Why parties and elections in authoritarian regimes?* Presented at Annual Meeting of the American Political Science Association, Washington, DC.

Giddens, A. (1994). *The constitution of society introduction of the theory of structuration.* University of California Press.

Glasius, M. (2018). What authoritarianism is ... and is not: A practice perspective. *International Affairs, 94*(3), 515–533.

Hale, H. (2014). *Patronal politics: Eurasian regime dynamics in comparative perspective.* Cambridge University Press.

Hoffmann, B. (2010). Bringing Hirschman back in: "Exit", "voice" and "loyalty" in the politics of transnational migration. *The Latin Americanist, 54*(2), 57–73.

Hooge, M., Marien, S., & Pauwels, T. (2011). Where do distrusting voters turn if there is no viable exit or voice option? The impact of political trust on electoral behaviour in the belgian regional elections of june 2009. *Government and Opposition, 46*(2), 245–273.

Hough, J. (1983). Pluralism, corporatism and the Soviet Union. In S. G. Solomon (Ed.), *Pluralism in the Soviet Union essays in honour of H. Gordon Skilling* (pp. 37–60). Macmillan Press.

Hirschman, A. (1993). Exit, voice, and the fate of the German democratic republic: An essay in conceptual history. *World Politics, 45*(2), 173–202.

Hirschman, A. (1970). *Exit, voice and loyalty: Responses to decline in firms, organizations and states.* Harvard University Press.

Isaacs, R. (2011). *Party system formation in Kazakhstan: Between formal and informal politics.* Routledge.

Ionescu, G., & de Madariaga, I. (1968). *Opposition: Past and present of a political institution.* C. A. Watts and Co. Ltd.

Kevlihan, R., & Ó Beacháin, D. (2017). Menus of manipulation: Authoritarian continuities in Central Asian elections. *Demokratizatsiya: The Journal of Post-Soviet Democratization, 25*(4), 407–434.

La Porte, J. (2014). Hidden in plain sight: Political opposition and hegemonic authoritarianism in Azerbaijan. *Post-Soviet Affairs, 31*(4), 339–366.

Landgrave, M., & Nowrasteh, A. (2016). Voice, exit, and liberty: The effect of emigration on origin country institutions. *Economic Development Bulletin, 25*, 1–4.

Langston, J. (2002). Breaking out is hard to do: Exit, voice, and loyalty in Mexico's one-party hegemonic regime. *Latin American Politics and Society, 44*(3), 61–88.

La Porte, J. (2017). Foreign versus domestic bribery: Explaining repression in kleptocratic regimes. *Comparative Politics, 50*(1), 83–102.

Linz, J. (2000). *Totalitarian and authoritarian regimes.* Lynne Rienner.

Lust-Okar, E. (2005). *Structuring conflict in the Arab world: Incumbents, opponents, and institutions.* Cambridge University Press.
Magaloni, B., & Kricheli, R. (2010). Political order and one-party rule. *The Annual Review of Political Science, 13,* 123–143.
Moses, W. (2005). Exit, vote and sovereignty: Migration, sates and globalization. *Review of International Political Economy, 12*(1), 53–77.
Noble, B. (2020). Authoritarian amendments: Legislative institutions as intraexecutive constraints in post-Soviet Russia. *Comparative Political Studies, 53*(9), 1417–1454.
O'Donnell, G. (1988). *Bureaucratic authoritarianism: Argentina, 1966–1973 in comparative perspective.* University of California Press.
O'Donnell, G., & Schmitter, P. (1986). *Transitions from authoritarian rule: Tentative conclusions about uncertain democracies* (Vol. 4). John Hopkins University Press.
Pepinsky, T. (2014). The institutional turn in comparative authoritarianism. *British Journal of Political Science, 44*(3), 631–653.
Pfaff, S., & Kim, H. (2003). Exit-voice dynamics in collective action: An analysis of emigration and protest in the East German revolution. *American Journal of Sociology, 109*(2), 401–444.
Reuter, J. O., & Robertson, G. (2015). Legislatures, cooptation, and social protest in contemporary authoritarian regimes. *The Journal of Politics, 77*(1), 235–248.
Ross, M. H. (1988). Political organization and political participation: Exit, voice and loyalty in pre-industrial societies. *Comparative Politics, 21*(1), 73–89.
Rustow, D. (1970). Transitions to democracy: Toward a dynamic model. *Comparative Politics, 2*(3), 337–363.
Schatz, E. (2009). The soft authoritarian tool kit: Agenda-setting power in Kazakhstan and Kyrgyzstan. *Comparative Politics, 41*(2), 203–222.
Schedler, A. (2002). The menu of manipulation. *Journal of Democracy, 13*(2), 36–50.
Schedler, A. (2006). *Electoral authoritarianism: The dynamics of unfree competition.* Lynne Rienner.
Schmitter, P. (1974). Still the century of corporatism? *The Review of Politics, 36*(1), 85–131.
Sippola, M. (2013). The awkward choices facing the baltic worker: Exit or loyalty. *Journal of Baltic Studies, 44*(4), 451–473.
Svolik, M. (2012). *The politics of authoritarian rule.* Cambridge University Press.
Williamson, S., & Magaloni, B. (2020). Legislatures and policy making in authoritarian regimes. *Comparative Political Studies, 53*(9), 1525–1543.
Witt, M. T. (2011). Exit, voice, loyalty revisited: Contours and implications for public administration in dark times. *Public Integrity, 13*(1), 239–251.

PART I

Opposition Agency and Opposition-Regime Relations in Authoritarianism

CHAPTER 2

Defining, Conceptualising and Theorising Opposition-Regime Relations in Authoritarian Regimes

Introduction

The meaning of political opposition in either a pluralistic or hegemonic context can be contingent on regime type. As the introduction noted, opposition exists in a dependent (even co-dependent) relationship with the regime. This means, as Jean Blondel argued, 'that the character of the opposition is tied to the character of the government' (Blondel, 1997, 463), a sentiment we will further consider when conceptualising regime-opposition equilibria. Furthermore, Robert Dahl's (1973, 9) well-grounded observation that 'differences in political preferences among the people of a country tend towards diversity and multiplicity rather than bipolarity', is indicative of the simple dichotomy of regime and opposition masking a profusion of oppositional forces and types (let alone regime factionalism). Of course, this leans towards the oft, overused, and clichéd expression that opposition is a difficult-to-define concept. To some extent, this is true, but only if we are seeking a general or universal definition which can be applied across varying types of political systems and different forms of regimes. Here, instead, the aim is more modest, to offer a conceptual and theoretical reading of political opposition which can be used in the case of Kazakhstan and perhaps the broader Eurasian space.

© The Author(s), under exclusive license to Springer Nature Switzerland AG 2022
R. Isaacs, *Political Opposition in Authoritarianism*, The Theories, Concepts and Practices of Democracy, https://doi.org/10.1007/978-3-031-06536-1_2

The analysis in this chapter explores two areas. Firstly, it seeks to develop a conceptualisation of opposition appropriate for the Kazakhstani case. The analysis will consider how political opposition has been defined and conceptualised in the classic political studies scholarship (mostly associated with polyarchies and democratic transition) and in more recent scholarship concerned with opposition in authoritarian contexts. The chapter argues that both in the classical literature, and largely in work which has analysed opposition in non-democratic contexts, political opposition is usually understood and framed in institutional terms, essentially in the form of political parties. Opposition conceptualised in this way is problematic in the authoritarian context (and Kazakhstan specifically) because the chances of political opposition becoming institutionalised are highly circumscribed. In the case of Kazakhstan, opposition parties do not have equitable or realistic chances of obtaining political office nor representation. Thus, to understand opposition in the case of Kazakhstan, and to make sense of the dynamics of in opposition, and in opposition-regime relations, it is necessary to return to a broader Dahlian definition of opposition which can account for a wider range of opposition actors beyond institutional opposition. The chapter puts forward a three-part typology for understanding different types of opposition actors in non-democratic contexts which includes individual forms of opposition (high-ranking individuals), organisational (political parties and public movements) and grassroots-based spontaneous opposition. Moreover, the chapter also argues in the case of Kazakhstan, and to some extent the broader Eurasian space, there is an oligarchic quality to opposition which needs to be considered.

The second focus of the chapter addresses how scholars of comparative authoritarianism have theorised two forms of opposition-regime equilibria. The first concerns the relationship between dissent and repression and the extent to which a rise in one can precipitate a rise in the other. The second is the way in which regime and opposition get locked into a co-dependent relationship via co-optation. As noted in the introduction, non-democratic rulers who view the opposition as a credible threat offer jobs, resources and other spoils to the opposition in exchange for support. These two models of regime-opposition equilibria reveal two notable findings. Firstly, there is a tendency to underplay the role of opposition agency in the regime-opposition relationship, and what impact opposition agency could have on regime dynamics. Secondly, the literature does not explain what happens when a regime views opposition as ambiguous and co-optation and power sharing is absent. The chapter concludes by arguing that the story of Kazakhstani opposition provides a puzzling case in this respect. The Kazakhstani regime under Nursultan Nazarbayev has reacted to opposition agency by treating institutional opposition ambiguously, rarely offering co-optation, but at the same time the regime has taken the opposition seriously by using coercive sanctions and institutional adaptation which marginalised and constricted the opposition's ability to act and compete electorally.

Defining Opposition

All political systems to some extent contain the expression and organisation of varied political preferences—even in totalitarian systems—it is part of our human condition to accumulate political preferences and seek to express them. As Dahl noted, 'during any given period, therefore, a political system will contain some people who, if there were no barriers or costs to their doing so, would be opposed to the conduct of the government' (Dahl, 1971, 2). Thus, political opposition is an integral human dynamic of authoritarian systems. However, its conceptualisation has often been nebulous (Norton, 2008, 236). Writing half a Century ago Rodney Barker (1971, 4) sought to highlight the varying meanings attached to the concept of opposition and how they were treated as different aspects of the same phenomenon rather than different though related phenomena. Barker identified at least six meanings for political opposition including total resistance to the state and a determination to overthrow by any means; resistance to the oppressive institutions of the state; resistance to the regime in control of the state (as distinct from the state itself) and a denial of their legitimacy; a loyal opposition which opposes the ruling regime, but does not contest their legitimacy; a system of constitutional checks and balances; and a more moderate attempt to modify the action of government without resorting to harsh condemnation (Barker, 1971, 5). As Norton (2008) has noted, these varying meanings can be easily channelled into two broad categories: those who oppose and challenge the legitimacy of the state and those who oppose but accept the legitimacy of the state and work within the existing parameters and rules of the game. This dichotomy mirrors other positions within the classic political studies literature on opposition such as Juan Linz's (1973) systemic versus non-systemic opposition and Sartori's

(1966) 'real' versus 'anti-system' opposition. Normatively underpinning these binaries is the distinction between a loyal constitutional opposition (this can be observed in terms such as in the UK of 'her majesty's loyal opposition') and a disloyal and unconstitutional opposition.

This binary definition of opposition reveals at least two issues with the classic approaches to the study of political opposition. Firstly, as evident in Barker's six meanings of opposition, there was a tendency to focus on the typologies and roles of political opposition (Brack & Weinblum, 2011). This typologising was most evident in the work of Dahl (1973, 2–4) and his distinction between polyarchies, near polyarchies, competitive oligarchies, hegemonies and near-hegemonic regimes. Dahl's typology of regimes is important not least as it represented the different potential modes of conflict between various groups within a society (Ionescu & de Madariaga, 1972, 8). Furthermore, with such public contestation being a central element of democratisation (Dahl, 1971, 10), the regime types provided a guide to how preferences can develop into 'systems of public contestation' as societies transform towards polyarchies (Dahl, 1971, 11–12). As such, this reveals the second issue with the classic literature on political opposition which is its highly normative nature. Dahl's focus on 'systems of public contestation' as important in transformations to polyarchies, highlights the way in which the study of political opposition was limited largely to that of democratic states. Political opposition, thus, was understood as a highly institutionalised phenomenon, what Ionescu and de Madariaga (1972, 9), described as 'the crowning institution of a fully institutionalised political society and those political societies which are variously called democratic, liberal, parliamentary, constitutional, pluralistic-constitutional, or even open or free'.

Thus, traditionally the study of political opposition had been aligned primarily, as Helms (2004, 24) writes, with a focus 'which usually tackles only the various manifestations of parliamentary opposition', which are often 'considered 'to be the 'true' form of opposition', while extra parliamentary forms are considered 'deviant'. Hence, un-institutionalised opposition is then often labelled as 'anti-system' when compared to the so-called 'real opposition' (Sartori, 1966). This illustrates the ways in which the institutionalisation of political opposition, typically in the form of parliamentary opposition, is considered an essential component not just of a functioning liberal democracy, but also as a crucial factor in democratic consolidation, being representative of the institutionalisation of regime accountability (Stepan, 1997). In polyarchies such institutional opposition represents an alternative government in waiting, and thus plays an important role in offering an alternative body of legislation (Brack & Weinblum, 2011, 71–72).

This focus primarily on the institutionalisation of political opposition (Ionescu & de Madariaga, 1968; Norton, 2008), tends to narrow the focus of what type of opposition actors are appropriate to study as legitimate oppositional agents (Brack & Weinblum, 2011). This is problematic in the case of authoritarian regimes where political opposition often has no realistic opportunity to be an alternative government. Rather, in authoritarian contexts, opposition tends to be actors outside of parliament who are still able to use extra-parliamentary tools to oppose the ruling regime (Brack & Weinblum, 2011, 73). Thus, any definition of opposition which is to be used in the context of studying authoritarian regimes must account for the fact that many opposition activities occur outside the framework of political parties (Blondel, 1997, 465).

Conceptualising Opposition in Authoritarian Systems

There are several consequences of this focus on institutional forms of political opposition (namely political parties) and a narrowing of the range of opposition actors under study. Firstly, once 'one moves from here to studying political oppositions in regimes beyond liberal democracy, established terms tend to lose their familiar meanings' (Helms, 2021, 2). As Ludger Helms (2021, 2) has argued, anti-system parties in democratic systems usually adopt agendas which challenge liberal democracy, while in authoritarian contexts such anti-system parties are typically (but not always) those committed to introducing democratic reform. This demonstrates the necessity of re-thinking how we approach and understand the study of opposition in authoritarian contexts.

Secondly, despite the need to approach opposition politics in authoritarian contexts in a different way, the focus of opposition activity in non-democratic contexts still tends towards institutionalisation and the competitive opportunities available to parties *vis-à-vis* electoral politics (Gelman, 2005; La Porte, 2014; Semenov, 2017; Shkel & Shakirova, 2014) and their eventual 'failure' when regimes deploy 'menus of manipulation' (Harvey, 2011; Kevlihan & Ó Beacháin, 2017; Schedler, 2002). Alternatively, studies have sought to examine opposition parties' efforts in the face of such structural constraints to develop alliances, coordination strategies and coalition-building to overcome the institutional barriers which undermine and impede their electoral success, contestability and even viability (Cavatora, 2009; Haugbølle & Cavatorta, 2011; Laštro & Bieber, 2021; Selçuk & Hekimci, 2020). Much of this literature represents a step forward in considering the agency of political opposition in non-democratic settings, something which will be discussed further below, and how political opposition use tools and strategies at their disposal to overcome regime-imposed structural constraints (Dettman, 2018). Thus, while there has been an effort to move beyond a regime-centred focus, the literature has still lent towards studying political opposition in authoritarian contexts in relation to their institutional opportunities in challenging the incumbent regime.

Thirdly, given in many authoritarian contexts political opposition has limited, if not non-existent, chances of obtaining representation in the legislature, there is perhaps a need to expand upon our understanding of what constitutes opposition actors in authoritarian sites. In other words, we need to move beyond parliamentary and party-based political opposition and be more sensitive to opposition beyond institutional boundaries. For example, Holger Albrecht argues, in the case of autocracies, that opposition needs to be understood as a procedural mechanism with organisational capacity which: engages in competitive interactions with the incumbent regime; has political professionals; financial support and which exists outside of the regime (2013). Thus, the emphasis for Albrecht is that even in non-democratic settings opposition should be viewed as movements or parties in contention with the regime. More recent literature has sought to demonstrate the wider range of opposition actors in authoritarian contexts. Sofie Bedford and Laurent Vinatier (2019) point to the role of social movements and activists (as well as electoral opposition) in contesting the Belarussian and Azerbaijani regimes, using media, education and lobbying as oppositional strategies. Other scholars have looked at the role of civil society groups and activists (Cavatorta, 2013), digital bloggers and social media activists (Gainous et al., 2018; Pearce & Hajizada, 2014), and even film directors and artists (Isaacs, 2018).

Expanding the scope of what constitutes opposition actors, while also making sense of the character and nature of political opposition in authoritarian settings, does illustrate the complexity of oppositional and contentious politics in authoritarian societies. Thus, among this complexity, how can we define and best conceptualise political opposition in authoritarian contexts? Robert Dahl's original definition of opposition from his 1966 work has framed much of the study of opposition politics, although it has been criticised for being too broad (Bedford & Vinatier, 2019; Brack & Weinblum, 2011; Schapiro, 1967). Dahl (1966, xvi) defined opposition as:

> Suppose that A determines the conduct of some aspect of the government of a particular political system during some interval … Suppose that during this interval B cannot determine the conduct of the government, and that B is opposed to the conduct of the government by A. Then B is what we mean by 'an opposition'.

In this way opposition is an emotional instinct rooted in human nature (Ionescu & de Madariaga, 1972, 6), which is 'logically, organically, and morphologically…the dialectical counterpart of power' (Ionescu & Madariaga, 1968, 10). Differently put, any given government (political party or otherwise) position exists in as much as there is a counter-position which acts to oppose. In other words, opposition can be understood as any agent which seeks to oppose the policy, governance and strategies of power. The broadness of Dahl's definition is attractive for its capacity to capture a variety of opposition actors—something necessary for the Kazakhstani case where political opposition manifests itself in a range of actors including political parties, trade unions, civic groups, street protests and even artists.

The conceptualisation of opposition in authoritarian systems has tended towards understanding opposition as the counterpoint to the regime, tying the character of the opposition to that of the regime (Dettman, 2018). As such, opposition-regime relations tend to mirror earlier theorising which categorised opposition in relation to their systemic or anti-systemic properties. For example, Albrecht (2013) established a typology for defining different types of opposition in authoritarian regimes which included regime-loyal opposition that works within the confines of the regime; a tolerated opposition; and an anti-system opposition. Likewise, Turovsky (2014, 13) observes, in the case of Russia, 'oppositionness' as a continuum whereby co-optation in (and support for) the regime ranges from zero to complete loyalty. While such an approach highlights the blurred boundaries that can exist between opposition parties and politicians, and the regime itself, in authoritarian contexts, it still reduces political opposition to those who might be considered professional politicians and institutionalised parties, leaving out extra-parliamentary, non-institutionalised social movement-based and civic forms of political opposition. Such a conceptualisation also leans heavily towards the power of the regime over opposition agency, given opportunities for electoral competitiveness and opposition co-optation (e.g., parliamentary representation in exchange for loyalty) are largely driven by regime agency.

Understanding and Defining Opposition in the Kazakhstani Case

So, how can we make sense of the above discussion on defining political opposition in authoritarian systems considering the case of Kazakhstan and the broader Eurasian space? As highlighted already, there are two key takeaways from the existing scholarship on political opposition in non-democratic contexts. Firstly, there has been a tendency to focus on an institutional conceptualisation of political opposition, one which pivots on opposition in the form of political parties which compete electorally to gain office. Consequently, less stress has been placed on other types of actors. Given the activities of political parties are highly constrained in authoritarian regimes, political opposition often emerges in non-institutional sites. Thus, it is important that non-institutional forms of political opposition are captured and analysed alongside institutional forms of opposition in such non-democratic contexts. Secondly, scholarship on political opposition in authoritarian systems has primarily, although not exclusively, focused on the agency of the regime *vis-à-vis* the opposition.

Much, but not all, of the scholarship which has addressed political opposition in the Eurasian space has generally followed this pattern with a general focus on political parties as the site of opposition, while also paying closer attention to regime rather than opposition agency. Most notably this can be observed in the cases of Russia (Hahn, 1994, March 2009), Belarus (Ash, 2015; Silitski, 2005), Kazakhstan (Junisbai & Junisbai, 2005; Kennedy, 2006) and Azerbaijan (Sultanova, 2014) to the extent that the lack of electoral success in Russia, at least, meant that opposition parties were a 'dying species' (Gelman, 2005). However, events from 2010 onwards, which saw a considerable increase in street protests, a wider array of civic-based opposition activists and the emergence of the Internet and social media as tools for opposition organisation, necessitated a shift in focus from party-based institutionalised opposition to examining the nexus between political and civic opposition (Gelman, 2015; White, 2015). This scholarly development is indicative of a trend across the Eurasian space where the enclosure of the formal institutional and electoral space for formal opposition parties meant that political opposition emerged in other more civic-based sites, through street protests (Evans, 2012; Koesel & Bunce, 2012), social media (Bode & Makarychev, 2013; Pearce, 2014) and what Bedford and Vinatier (2019) termed 'resistance models'—that is where political opposition emerges through different tactics such as lobbying, education and the media. Kazakhstan has broadly followed this pattern. For the first two decades of independence since 1991, political parties formed what would be considered 'the opposition' to the Nazarbayev regime. But the gradual marginalisation of opposition parties, and their removal from the political scene has meant that political opposition in Kazakhstan has found voice in more non-institutional spaces. This book is the story of that shift from institutional to non-institutional opposition in the country—and how the dynamic agency of opposition as part of that shift has contributed to shaping regime outcomes.

Therefore, to study political opposition in Kazakhstan, its agency and its relationship to the regime, a definition is required which captures both institutional and non-institutional forms of opposition to account for the dynamic nature of opposition politics in the country over the last thirty years. It is for this reason that I return to a Dahlian definition of political opposition which constitutes any expression which disagrees with government policy and action. Such a definitional position assists in capturing a broader range of agents and sites of political opposition that can be found in authoritarian regimes, and in Kazakhstan specifically, allowing us to sidestep the normativity of conceptualising political opposition only considering its constitutional and institutional role and with a less determinative position for the regime *vis-à-vis* opposition. However, this is not to suggest that more institutional forms of political opposition in Kazakhstan such as political parties are not important, in fact they have been central to the story of political opposition in the country. Rather, the important thing to note is that it is necessary to widen the analytical scope of what is considered political opposition in Kazakhstan to pay closer attention to how the nature and dynamics of political opposition has changed over time in the country and how opposition agency has shaped regime-opposition relations. This may not be a definition which is appropriate for all cases of opposition, not least in established liberal democracies where the tendency is to understand opposition in only institutional terms.

Three-Part Typology of Opposition Actors

This study proposes a three-part typology of potential opposition actors that accounts for the diverse forms of political opposition appearing in authoritarian contexts and in Kazakhstan specifically. The first is to see political opposition at the level of the *individual*. This could be a single high-profile elite figure, a former minister or oligarchic business figure, who has the resources to mobilise a movement or political party on their behalf with the aim of challenging the incumbent regime. It could also simply refer to individual civil or rights activists or even journalists who seek to expose and confront autocratic regime policies. Such non-elite individuals might not possess the resources to establish a broad-based organisational movement to mobilise support for their campaign against the regime. Nonetheless, through their activism they can bring to light issues and deficiencies with the regime—and can provide a sustained challenge to authoritarian rule by broadening the scope of regime critique in the public discourse and imagination.

The second type of opposition actor we can identify operates at the *organisational* level. This would include any political movement which possesses a coordinated organisational structure and resources to mobilise against the regime either by contesting seats for election at the national and local level, organising protests or public policy campaigns in relation to specific issues where the regime is understood to be deficient or by seeking to change regime policy through advice, report writing or advocacy. Political parties, trade unions, religious groups, non-governmental organisations and newspapers would fall under this category of organisational opposition (although this list is not exhaustive). There is, of course, some fluidity across *individual* and *organisational* types of opposition in authoritarianism. As alluded to above, individuals (often elite or ex-government members, but not necessarily) will often establish political parties or even civil society organisations to mobilise support for their cause against the regime. As will be analysed later in this book, in the case of Kazakhstan, numerous oligarchic former members of the elite exited the confines of the regime to challenge the incumbency of the then president, Nursultan Nazarbayev, and created political parties as the organisational conduits to mobilise popular support.

The final type of opposition actor can be understood as more grounded in *grassroots*-based civic forms of activism. These forms of opposition can seemingly take on a spontaneous character but are largely driven and organised through what Bennett and Segerberg (2012) termed 'connective action' where digital media becomes a central element of organising contentious politics. Such forms of civic-based grassroots activism, structured through digital and social media, have been present in numerous high-profile examples of political opposition against authoritarian regimes, from street protests and political blogging in Russia (Bode & Makarychev, 2013; White, 2015), to the Arab Spring (Markham, 2014), student protests in the UK (Hensby, 2017) and the Umbrella Movement in Hong Kong (Cheng & Chan, 2017). As will be discussed later in this book, the Kazakhstani regime has been subject to numerous spontaneous grassroots-based forms of contentious politics which have challenged the regime in both explicit and implicit ways, although not to the extent that any of the events in 2011, 2016, 2019 and 2022, represented a tipping point for regime change. And, while digital networks of 'connective action' have played a significant coordinating role in some of these events, what is more revealing about the Kazakhstani case is what grassroots-based political opposition explains about the internal workings of the political regime in Kazakhstan and the mutually constitutive relationship between regime and opposition. As will be discussed below, spontaneous grassroots-based opposition appears as a sudden surprise because of the breakdown of feedback loops that can exist in regime-opposition equilibria when the regime fails to get the balance right between sanctioning and co-opting individual and organisational forms of political opposition.

This threefold typology of opposition actors in and under authoritarianism is not exhaustive. The categories are drawn broadly to address the need to account for a wider array of opposition actors in non-democratic settings. Nonetheless, the purpose here is to use this typology as an interpretative frame to analyse the agency of opposition actors in Kazakhstan. With this conceptual account of opposition in authoritarianism in hand, and a clearer sense of the types of opposition actors involved, it is worth turning attention to conceptually framing the relationship between regime and opposition.

Theorising Regime-Opposition Relations in Authoritarianism

Leonard Schapiro (1967) suggested that regime and opposition are uncomfortable bedfellows. While on the surface this seems a glib sentiment, it does speak to the important fact that regime and opposition are tied together in a mutually constitutive relationship. Regime and opposition are tethered together and understanding this equilibrium is key to understanding the logic of opposition in authoritarian systems.

Broadly speaking the literature on comparative authoritarianism alerts us to two forms of regime-opposition equilibria. The first concerns the relationship between dissent and repression. Repression sparks dissident behaviour and dissident behaviour sparks repression, even if the relationship between the two is dependent upon context and timing (Maher & Petterson, 2008; Moore, 1998). The relationship between opposition and regime in this form of equilibrium is driven by imitative behaviour. As Sabine Carey (2006, 3) noted:

> If the population is faced with repression, the citizens are most likely to respond with dissent. Similarly, if the government encounters protest, it is expected to respond with repression. The government and the opposition orientate their actions primarily on the observable behaviour of the opponent because the situation under which both actors operate is marked by limited information, limited capabilities, and uncertain payoffs.

This form of regime-opposition equilibrium has many variations. Politically insulated personalist regimes tend to adopt more coercive behaviour to protect themselves from the discontent of the wider population, while those which use political institutions such as parties or legislatures can channel political dissent through institutional mechanisms, and thus have less necessity to apply coercive practices (Davenport, 2007, 486–487). However, some studies have shown that regimes which use institutional co-optation are more incentivised to adopt individualised repressions (Frantz & Kendall-Taylor, 2014). Nevertheless, whatever the strategic use of *how* and *when* the regime applies repression (Bashin & Gandhi, 2013), the relationship between regime and opposition can be observed as a reciprocal one where 'governments and dissidents choose their action in participation of each other's behaviour' (Hencken Ritter & Conrad, 2016).

The second form of regime-opposition equilibrium is broader in scope and rooted in the 'institutional turn' in comparative authoritarianism (Pepinsky, 2014). Studies have illustrated how formal institutions such as parties and legislatures allow authoritarian leaders to monitor competing elite groups to prevent internal conflict, offer policy concessions to key oppositional groups and co-opt rival elites through the distribution of resources and rents (Gandhi, 2008, xvii–xvx ; Malesky & Schuler, 2010; Reuter & Robertson, 2015, 236; Svolik, 2012). These strategies of authoritarian rulers solve two dilemmas: to prevent their legitimacy being undermined and to ensure cooperation with their rule (Gandhi, 2008, xvii). Consequently, authoritarian regimes which use legislatures and parties to co-opt and offer policy concessions to potential oppositional elites are viewed to be more durable (Geddes, 2003). Thus, an equilibrium exists where an authoritarian leader is dependent upon elite rivals and opposition groups to support, legitimise and stabilise their rule. Conversely, opposition becomes dependent upon the regime for spoils, rents and policy concessions.

This is not, however, a uniform relationship and the extent to which the regime offers policy concessions or rents depends on the resources available and type of opposition. For instance, authoritarian leaders respond differently depending on how the opposition is incorporated into the regime (Conrad, 2011, 1168). Opposition located within the legislature will receive material concessions from the regime, while those situated outside the legislature will be in receipt of policy concessions (Conrad, 2011). Moreover, the extent of co-optation is dependent upon the resources available. As Jennifer Gandhi and Grant Buckles have argued, 'incumbents do not have infinite resources with which they can co-opt opposition elites, and in fact, the use of these resources for opposition co-optation can be costly' (Gandhi & Buckles, 2016, 1). Therefore, for regimes to use valuable resources to co-opt opposition, the incumbent needs to perceive of the opposition as a 'credible' threat that could engender wider social protest or an elite-led *coup-d'état* (Gandhi & Buckles, 2016; Magaloni, 2008). An authoritarian leader, therefore, channels valuable revenues, often accrued from external rents, to bribe and split the opposition when faced with a credible challenge to the regime (Wright, 2008). At the same time, the opposition also possesses agency. As Buckles notes, not all credible threats are successfully co-opted and parties with a less vibrant activist base are more likely to be co-opted, because leaders of parties with a large activist base face the threat of rebellion and resistance from activists if they acquiesce to the regime or if the price of co-optation is not significant enough (Buckles, 2019).

There are two significant things of note in this body of literature for our purposes. Firstly, although the literature concerns opposition-regime relations, most of the focus remains on the agency of the regime *vis-à-vis* the opposition. On the one hand this makes sense, given the inequitable power relationship between the two interlocutors. But, on the other hand, as Buckles' (2019) research has demonstrated, there can be an analytical pay off when attention is equally paid to that of opposition agency. Secondly, what is also significant about this body of literature is that regime and opposition are observed as existing in a co-dependent relationship. The regime relies on the opposition for survival and legitimacy and the opposition relies on the regime for rents and concessions. But the literature suggests that this equilibrium exists only if the opposition can be viewed as a credible threat by the regime. What the literature does not account for is when the credibility of the opposition is understood as ambiguous by the regime and co-optation and power sharing either fails or does not take place at all and this is where the relationship between the opposition and regime in Kazakhstan makes for a puzzling case.

The Opposition in Kazakhstan: A Brief Profile

In Kazakhstan, like many Eurasian states, the opposition which has appeared since the inception of the state in 1991 is by and large institutional: political parties and formal political organisations seeking to gain access to state institutions, whether parliamentary seats, local councils or the presidential office. However, as will be discussed in later chapters, like the case of Russia in recent years, the decline of formal institutional opposition has led to broader grassroots opposition to the regime (Alexander, 2018; Dubuisson, 2020; Gelman, 2015; Nasimova et al., 2019; Satpayev & Umbetaliyeva, 2015). From 1998, political opposition in Kazakhstan possessed an oligarchic quality. Political opposition became centred on elite figures who previously served in the government and who possessed independent financial means largely accrued through the privatisation process of the 1990s. This oligarchic opposition emerged because of disaffection with the distribution of spoils within the regime, which mostly benefited members of the president's family. Consequently, these oligarchies went into opposition, creating political parties to represent their interests (Isaacs, 2011; Junisbai, 2010; Peyrouse, 2012). Individuals such as former Prime Minister Akezhan Kazhegeldin, former presidential advisor and parliamentary deputy Bolat Abilov, and former Energy Minister and owner of Bank Turan Alem (BTA)[1] Mukhtar Ablyazov, comprised a non-systemic form of opposition which sought the removal of the Nazarbayev regime and a shift towards liberal democratic forms of governance.

There are two significant things we can draw from the example of the opposition in Kazakhstan. Firstly, the emergence of this oligarchic political opposition illustrates a failure of co-optation on the part of the regime. President Nazarbayev failed to assuage opposition elites' anxieties regarding the distribution of resources alongside broader concerns pertaining to the development of regime (Junisbai & Junisbai, 2005). Such a failure is not a consequence of a lack of resources, given the regime is resource rich (Kazakhstan is an oil and gas wealthy country) (Global Witness, 2012). Existing scholarship might explain this lack of co-optation because of the non-credible threat of the opposition. However, the Nazarbayev regime took the 'threat' of this oligarchic opposition seriously enough to seek to protect itself from its emergence by engaging in considerable institutional adaptation to lock the opposition out of the electoral process, while also applying coercive sanctions against individual leaders, their organisations and supporters (Isaacs, 2011, Kevlihan & Ó Beacháin, 2017).

The second aspect to note is that if we focus on the agency of opposition this ambiguity of the Kazakhstani opposition highlights a different form of regime-opposition equilibrium. The study of opposition in authoritarian contexts gains a great deal when the analytical attention shifts to a focus on the agency of opposition, rather than just the strategies and practices of the regime (Albrecht, 2013; Bedford & Vinatier, 2019; Pfaff & Kim, 2003). It allows us to understand how the relationship between opposition and regime can contribute to regime stability or instability. And the case of the Kazakhstani opposition is revealing as it illustrates a dynamic and paradoxical equilibrium between regime and opposition. Albert Hirschman's frame of exit, voice and loyalty can help explain how the Nazarbayev regime reacted to variants of opposition agency by applying sanctions and modifying the institutional environment

---

[1] BTA is one of Kazakhstan's largest banks.

to shore up its position. However, on the one hand, curtailing opposition agency through sanctions and institutional adaptation strengthened the regime against such threats, but on the other such actions limited feedback signals regarding the regime's performance leading to intensive dissatisfaction among the broader public which brought 'shocks' to regime stability via spontaneous, grassroots forms of opposition, most significantly in 2011, 2016, 2019 and 2022.

Conclusion

This chapter has argued that in the case of Kazakhstan it is necessary to conceive of political opposition in a broad Dahlian fashion as a phenomenon which can consist of both institutional and non-institutional actors. From the perspective of the case of Kazakhstan, this study frames opposition actors by way of three categories: individual, organisational and grassroots, although this is not an exhaustive list. At the same time, this chapter has argued that existing theoretical models of regime-opposition relations do not take close enough account of opposition agency nor how a regime might adopt an ambiguous approach to opposition credibility. The question this leaves is: how can we best conceptualise opposition agency and relations in the Kazakhstani case to draw out its theoretical and conceptual contribution to our wider understanding of comparative authoritarianism? The following chapter seeks to answer this question by conceptualising opposition agency and this mutually constitutive relationship between the opposition and regime in Kazakhstan by drawing upon Hirschman's framework of exit, voice and loyalty.

References

Albrecht, H. (2013). *Raging against the machine: Political opposition under authoritarianism in Egypt*. Syracuse University Press.

Alexander, C. (2018). Homeless in the homeland: Housing protests in Kazakhstan. *Critique of Anthropology, 38*(2), 204–220.

Ash, K. (2015). The election trap: The cycle of postelectoral repression and opposition fragmentation in Lukashenko's Belarus. *Democratization, 22*(6), 1030–1053.

Barker, R. (1971). Introduction. In R. Barker (Ed.), *Studies in opposition* (pp. 1–30). Palgrave Macmillan.

Bashin, T., & Gandhi, J. (2013). Timing and targeting of state repression in authoritarian elections. *Electoral Studies, 32*, 620–631.

Bedford, S., & Vinatier, L. (2019). Resisting the irresistible: 'Failed opposition' in Azerbaijan and Belarus revisited. *Government and Opposition, 54*(4), 686–714.

Bennett, W., & Segerberg, A. (2012). The logic of connective action. *Information, Communication & Society, 15*(5), 739–768.

Blondel, J. (1997). Political opposition in the contemporary world. *Government and Opposition, 32*(2), 462–486.

Bode, N., & Makarychev, A. (2013). The new social media in Russia. *Problems of Post-Communism, 60*(2), 53–62.

Brack, N., & Weinblum, S. (2011). Political opposition: Towards a new research agenda. *Interdisciplinary Political Studies, 1*(1), 69–78.

Buckles, G. (2019). Internal opposition dynamics and restraints on authoritarian control. *British Journal of Political Science, 49*(3), 883–900.

Carey, S. (2006). The dynamic relationship between protest and repression. *Political Research Quarterly, 59*(1), 1–12.

Cavatorta, F. (2013). *Civil society activism under authoritarian rule: A comparative perspective*. Routledge.

Cavatorta, F. (2009). 'Divided they stand, divided they fail': Opposition politics in Morocco. *Democratization, 16*(1), 137–156.

Conrad, C. (2011). Constrained concessions: Beneficent dictatorial responses to the domestic political opposition. *International Studies Quarterly, 55*(4), 1167–1187.

Dahl, R. A. (Ed.). (1966). *Political oppositions in Western democracies*. Yale University Press.

Dahl, R. A. (1971). *Polyarchies: Participation and opposition*. Yale University Press.

Dahl, R. A. (1973). Introduction. In R. A. Dahl (Ed.), *Regimes and oppositions* (pp. 1–26). Yale University Press.

Davenport, C. (2007). State repression and the tyrannical peace. *Journal of Peace Research, 44*(4), 485–504.

Dettman. (2018). *Dilemmas of opposition: Building parties and coalitions in authoritarian regimes*. Ph.D. dissertation. Cornell University.

Dubuisson, E. (2020). Whose world? Discourses of protection for land, environment, and natural resources in Kazakhstan. *Problems of Post-Communism*. https://doi.org/10.1080/10758216.2020.1788398

Evans, A. (2012). Protests and civil society in Russia: The struggle for the Khimki forest. *Communist and Post-Communist Studies, 45*(3–4), 233–242.

Frantz, E., & Kendall-Taylor, A. (2014). A dictator's toolkit: Understanding how co-optation affects repression in autocracies. *Journal of Peace Research, 51*(3), 332–346.

Gainous, J., Wagner, K., & Ziegler, C. (2018). Digital media and political opposition in authoritarian systems: Russia's 2011 and 2016 Duma elections. *Democratization, 25*(2), 209–226.

Gandhi, J. (2008). *Political institutions under dictatorship*. Cambridge University. Press.

Gandhi, J., & Buckles, G. (2016, April 7–10). *Opposition unity and co-optation in hybrid regimes*. Paper Presented at the Annual Midwest Political Science Association Conference, Chicago, IL, pp. 1–33.

Gelman, V. (2005). Political opposition in Russia: A dying species? *Post-Soviet Affairs, 21*(3), 226–246.

Global Witness. (2012). *Risky business: Kazakhstan, Kazakhmys PLC and the London Stock Exchange*. Global Witness.

Hahn, G. (1994). Opposition politics in Russia. *Europe-Asia Studies, 46*(2), 305–355.

Harvey, C. (2011). Changes in the menu of manipulation: Electoral fraud, ballot stuffing, and voter pressure in the 2011 Russian election. *Electoral Studies, 41*(3), 105–117.

Haugbølle, R. H., & Cavatorta, F. (2011). Will the real Tunisian opposition please stand up? Opposition coordination failures under authoritarian constraints. *British Journal of Middle Eastern Studies, 38*(3), 323–341.

Helms, L. (2004). Five ways of institutionalizing political opposition: Lessons from the advanced democracies. *Government and Opposition, 39*(1), 22–54.

Helms, L. (2021). Introduction: The nature of political opposition in contemporary electoral democracies and autocracies. *European Political Science, 20*(April), 569–579.

Hensby, A. (2017). Open networks and secret Facebook groups: Exploring cycle effects on activists' social media use in the 2010/11 UK student protests. *Social Movement Studies, 16*(4), 466–478.

Hencken Ritter, E., & Conrad, C. R. (2016). Preventing and responding to dissent: The observational challenges of explaining strategic repression. *American Political Science Review, 110*(1), 85–99.

Ionescu, G., & de Madariaga, I. (1968). *Opposition: Past and present of a political institution*. C. A. Watts and Co. Ltd.

Ionescu, G., & de Madariaga, I. (1972). *Opposition: Past and present of a political institution*. Penguin Books, Ltd.

Isaacs, R. (2011). *Party system formation in Kazakhstan: Between formal and informal politics*. Routledge.

Isaacs, R. (2018). *Film and identity in Kazakhstan: Soviet and post-Soviet culture*. I.B. Tauris.

Junisbai, B. (2010). A tale of two Kazakhstans: Sources of political cleavage and conflict in the post-soviet period. *Europe-Asia Studies, 62*(2), 235–269.

Junisbai, B., & Junisbai, A. (2005). The democratic choice of Kazakhstan: A case study in economic liberalization, intra-elite cleavage and political opposition. *Demokratizatsiya: the Journal of Post-Soviet Democratization, 13*(2), 373–392.

Kennedy, R. (2006). A Colorless election: The 2005 presidential election in Kazakhstan, and what it means for the future of the opposition. *Problems of Post Communism, 53*(6), 46–58.

Kevlihan, R., & Ó Beacháin, D. (2017). Menus of manipulation: Authoritarian continuities in Central Asian elections. *Demokratizatsiya: The Journal of Post-Soviet Democratization, 25*(4), 407–434.

Koesel, K., & Bunce, V. (2012). Putin, popular protests, and political trajectories in Russia: A comparative perspective. *Post-Soviet Affairs, 28*(4), 403–423.

Maher, T., & Peterson, L. (2008). Time and country variation in contentious politics: Multilevel modelling of dissent and repression. *International Journal of Sociology, 38*(3), 52–81.

Malesky, E., & Schuler, P. (2010). Nodding or needling: Analyzing delegate responsiveness in an authoritarian parliament. *American Political Science Review, 104*(3), 482–502.

Moore, M. (1998). Repression and dissent: Substitution, context, and timing. *American Journal of Political Science, 42*(3), 851–873.

Nasimova, G. O., Buzurtanova, M. M., & Saitova, N. A. (2019). Social protests in Kazakhstan: Factors and trends. *Philosophy and Conflict Studies, 35*(3), 472–484.

Norton, P. (2008). Making sense of opposition. *The Journal of Legislative Studies, 14*(1–2), 236–250.

Laštro, C., & Bieber, F. (2021). The performance of opposition parties in competitive authoritarian regimes: Three case studies from the Western Balkans. *European Political Science, 20*(March), 617–629.

La Porte, J. (2014). Hidden in plain sight: Political opposition and hegemonic authoritarianism in Azerbaijan. *Post-Soviet Affairs, 31*(4), 339–366.

Linz, J. J. (1973). Opposition in and under Authoritarian regime: The case of Spain. In R. Dahl (Ed.), *Regimes and oppositions* (pp. 171–259). Yale University Press.

Pearce, K. (2014). Two can play at that game: Social media opportunities in Azerbaijan for government and opposition. *Demokratizatsiya, 22*(1), 39–66.

Pearce, K., & Hajizada, A. (2014). No laughing matter humor as a means of dissent in the digital era: The case of authoritarian Azerbaijan. *Demokratizatsiya, 22*(1), 67–85.

Pepinsky, T. (2014). The institutional turn in comparative authoritarianism. *British Journal of Political Science, 44*(3), 631–653.

Peyrouse, S. (2012). The Kazakh Neopatrimonial regime: Balancing uncertainties among the "family," oligarchs and technocrats. *Demokratizatsiya, 20*(4), 345–370.

Pfaff, S., & Kim, H. (2003). Exit-voice dynamics in collective action: An analysis of emigration and protest in the East German revolution. *American Journal of Sociology, 109*(2), 401–444.

Reuter, J. O., & Robertson, G. (2015). Legislatures, cooptation, and social protest in contemporary authoritarian regimes. *The Journal of Politics, 77*(1), 235–248.

Sartori, G. (1966). Opposition and control problems and prospects. *Government and Opposition, 1*(1), 149–154.

Satpayev, D., & Umbetaliyeva, T. (2015). The protests in Zhanaozen and the Kazakh oil sector: Conflicting interests in a Rentier State. *Journal of Eurasian Studies, 6*(2), 122–129.

Schapiro, L. (1967). Putting the lid on Leninism: Opposition and dissent in the communist one-party states. *Government and Opposition, 2*(2), 181–203.

Schedler, A. (2002). The menu of manipulation. *Journal of Democracy, 13*(2), 36–50.

Semenov, A. (2017). Against the stream: Political opposition in the Russian regions during the 2012–2016 electoral cycle. *Demokratizatsiya, 25*(4), 481–502.

Selçuk, O., & Hekimci, D. (2020). The rise of the democracy—Authoritarianism cleavage and opposition coordination in Turkey (2014–2019). *Democratization, 27*(8), 1496–1514.

Shkel, S., & Shakirova, E. V. (2014). Political opposition in the hybrid regime: Post-Soviet Russia experience. *Review of Political Science, 1*, 4–21.

Silitski, V. (2005). Preempting democracy: The case of Belarus. *Journal of Democracy, 16*(4), 83–97.

Stepan, A. (1997). Democratic opposition and democratization theory. *Government and Opposition, 32*(4), 657–663.

Sultanova, S. (2014). Challenging the Aliyev regime: Political opposition in Azerbaijan. *Demokratizatsiya, 22*(1), 15–37.

Svolik, M. (2012). *The politics of authoritarian rule*. Cambridge University Press.

Turovsky, R. (2014). Opposition parties in hybrid regimes: Between repression and co-optation: The case of Russia's regions. *Perspectives on European Politics and Society, 15*(1), 68–87.

White, D. (2015). Political opposition in Russia: The challenges of mobilisation and the political-civil society nexus. *East European Politics, 31*(3), 314–325.

Wright, J. (2008). Do authoritarian institutions constrain? How legislatures affect economic growth and investment. *American Journal of Political Science, 52*(2), 322–343.

CHAPTER 3

Exit, Voice and Loyalty: An Analytical Framework for Opposition Agency in Authoritarian Regimes

This chapter offers an analytical framework based on Albert Hirschman's treatise of exit, voice and loyalty for considering opposition agency in authoritarian political systems and for understanding equilibria between opposition and regime. After it was published in 1970, Albert Hirschman's *Exit, Voice and Loyalty*, became a cause célèbre, attracting widespread acclaim. Despite its initial application within the field of economics, Hirschman's frame was applied widely across scholarly disciplines, not least in political science. At the heart of Hirschman's framework is the dichotomy between exit and voice. In his own words 'there are two main types of activist reactions to discontent to which one belongs or with which one does business: either to voice one's complaints, while continuing as a member or customer, in the hope of improving matters; or exit from the organization, to take one's business elsewhere' (Hirschman, 1993, 173). Thus, exit and voice act as a corrective mechanism and are fundamental to a firm's survival and ability to retain a stable or dominant position within the marketplace.

Ordinarily, Hirschman did not see the model as applying to states, as voice and exit often acted as a safety valve rather than an incentive to reform (Brubaker, 1990, 13). However, the events of 1989 and the collapse of communism illustrated that in fact exit, voice and loyalty was highly applicable to political systems, not least in the case of revolution in the former East German state which was driven by the 'intensifying and mutually reinforcing pressures of exit and voice' (Brubaker, 1990, 13). Hirschman himself applied the framework to analyse the extent to which exit enabled or undermined voice in the German Democratic Republic and how this contributed to its collapse (Hirschman, 1993). Therefore, exit was used to conceptualise and understand migration from authoritarian states.

The correlation between exit and regime collapse, however, was complicated by studies which found that the relationship between exit and voice was more dynamic than previously thought. Steven Pfaff and Hyojoung Kim (2003, 438), for example, found that outward migration in the GDR provided both a signal of grievance against the regime and a weakening of opposition back home because it siphoned away prospective opposition activists. At the same time, migration as a form of exit has been demonstrated to impact on stabilising authoritarian regimes as it can make governments more responsive to the needs of citizens (Moses, 2005). Such interpretations of the relationship between exit and regime stability can also be further complicated by transnational migration, whereby the stark choice between exit and voice is observed not as mutually exclusive, but rather as overlapping and simultaneous (Hoffmann, 2010, 68). Furthermore, the expanding nature of authoritarian power beyond the borders of the state, through digital technology or specific participatory institutions, means that exit for dissidents is not as clear cut as previously assumed, given the power autocratic regimes have in punishing those who have left as well as cutting off contact with those dissidents who remain in the country (Dalmasso, 2018; Michaelsen, 2018).

The analysis in this book adds to the complexity of Hirschman's exit, voice and loyalty framework, especially in relation to non-democratic contexts. Rather than focus on outward migration as a form of opposition agency which shapes regime responses, this study on political opposition in Kazakhstan takes elite exit and voice as a starting point (which then leads to a broader exhibition of voice from the population). It follows the work of Joy Langston (2002) which has illustrated how elite exit served to strengthen Mexico's Institutional Revolutionary Party's (PRI) grip on power as it provided a signal to adapt and strengthen the institutions of power creating regime stability through an equilibrium built on co-optation. As Langston notes (2002, 65) the case of the PRI demonstrates how:

Elite ruptures were, without a doubt, the aggregate result of individual-level strategies; and both the exits and the regime's reaction to them caused evolutionary institutional change, which in turn brought about long-term political stability in the form of a one-party hegemonic state. Thus, political institutions in Mexico, such as restrictive party registration rules, candidate selection procedures, a sub- servient party, and a controlled cabinet, can be seen as the result of strategic bargaining and exits in a context of structural realities that influenced the strategies (exit, voice, or loyalty) of relevant actors.

To some extent, political elites follow a similar pattern in terms of their exit from the Nazarbayev regime in Kazakhstan. High-level elites sought to use a combination of exit and voice as a strategic bargaining tool to achieve some form of shift in government policy and more purposively a benefit to their position. The use of opposition agency in this form only served, on the surface, to strengthen the institutions and mechanisms of authoritarian rule, not dissimilar to Langston's argument in the case of the PRI in Mexico. Where the case of Kazakhstan departs from that of the PRI in terms of exit and voice, is the way in which high-level elite exit and voice, while seemingly foreclosing the chance of reform, as the regime uses opposition agency to strengthen its internal institutional mechanisms for managing parties, elections, and public protest, in fact serves to embolden non-elite voice. This, as this essay will later demonstrate, is partly a consequence of the ambiguous nature of high-level oligarchic elite opposition threat to the regime.

Following Pfaff and Kim (2003), the case of Kazakhstani elite exit into opposition also illustrates the dynamic relationship between exit and voice. The case of political opposition in Kazakhstan demonstrates that exit and voice is not a straightforward binary choice, as elite opposition agency can entail simultaneous exit and voice. Additionally, and even more significantly, as Dowding et al. (2000) have argued, there are multiple forms of exit and voice available in political settings. Thus, conceptualising opposition agency via the strategies of exit and voice needs to take account of the different options available for opposition elites. It is not a simple choice of exit versus voice versus loyalty. Rather there are different nodal points where exit, voice and loyalty can be used singularly or in pairs (i.e., exit and voice or exit and loyalty together). Thus, adopting the exit, voice and loyalty frame in the case of Kazakhstani political opposition allows us to unpack the greater complexity that exists in the strategies of political opposition when it comes to decisions of whether to exit the regime, activate voice or stay loyal or a combination of these options. Furthermore, such decisions on whether to use exit, voice or loyalty are dependent on the type of opposition (institutional vs. non-institutional) and the context within which it occurs. In other words, the extent to which opposition chooses to exit or use voice, or any combination of the different forms of exit and voice, is also conditioned by the ongoing response from the regime in terms of sanctions and institutional adaptation.

What follows in the rest of this chapter is the setting out of the exit, voice and loyalty framework for analysing opposition agency in Kazakhstan. The first part conceptualises exit, voice and loyalty as a form of opposition agency by considering the different forms and combinations of exit and voice which can exist. The second part focuses on how loyalty, sanctions and institutional adaptation influence the choice of exit and voice. And, finally, the third part conceptualises the nature of the opposition-regime equilibrium based on the exit, voice and loyalty framework when the opposition threat is ambiguous. The section outlines four different nodal points within the equilibrium where political opposition possesses agency in the form of exit, voice and loyalty. It then outlines the mutually constituted cycle of regime-opposition relations which underpins the equilibrium and establishes a paradox where at one and the same time the regime is both stable and unstable.

Exit and Voice

At its heart Hirschman's dichotomy between exit and voice is simple. In response to a deterioration of an organisation's performance members have a choice to stop buying the firm's products and/or leave the organisation (exit) or, alternatively express their dissatisfaction directly to the management or to some authority which management is subordinate or through general protest (voice) (Hirschman, 1970, 4). The key for the business is to then react to the revenue loss and develop a corrective strategy. Thus, exit acts as a crucial function for businesses by sending a signal to firms that it needs to react and adapt to perceived declines in quality and efficiency. Such a feedback mechanism is fundamental to a firm's survival and ability to retain a stable or dominant position within the marketplace.[1]

When applied to the context of states (and/or for the purpose of this book, authoritarian regimes) a similar logic applies. If we wish to understand something about state (or authoritarian) stability then we should examine the feedback effect of exit on the state or regime and the extent to which it reacts 'in such a manner as to remedy its weaknesses and inefficiencies' (Hirschman, 1993, 178). If a business firm relies on exit or voice as a signal to ensure survival it can also apply to an authoritarian regime to ensure regime durability. The action of either exit or voice by opposition elites creates pressure on authoritarian governments to react. Thus, in closed political systems exit and voice function as important signals regarding the perception of the diminishment of governmental quality (partly related to the quality of democratic governance). It enables an authoritarian regime to recuperate their position *vis-à-vis* their monopoly of power and policy. However, while exit might be an efficient means of signalling consumer demands in perfect markets, in instances where there is a monopoly of supply, as is the case in authoritarian political systems, it could be interpreted that consumers/opposition elites have nowhere to go (Dowding et al., 2000, 471). We need, therefore, to think about the type of exit and voice which are possible in authoritarian settings. This variation includes the choice to exit the regime[2] in the first instance, either with or without public voice, followed by the choice to exit the political system/country, again with the choice to do so with or without voice. These variations are discussed in more detail below.

As already alluded, 'to resort to voice, rather than exit, is for the customer or member to try changing the practices, policies, and outputs of the firm from which one buys or of the organization [sic] to which one belongs' (Hirschman, 1970, 30). Many who have followed Hirschman have pointed to the various modes of voice which exist. Dowding

---

[1] Hirschman argues that the relationship between the exit function and reaction function is variable in that if demand is inelastic with respect to a decline in quality, then the losses will be minimal to the firm, and they will not register the feedback mechanism from the impact of exit. However, if demand is too elastic then the reaction strategy will not take place as the firm will be wiped out with losses before it can respond. Thus, Hirschman posits that for exit to work best for the firm it requires both alert and inert customers. See Hirschman (1970, 22–25) for more detail.

[2] This assumes that in the case of authoritarian regimes, opposition elites tend to emerge from the regime in the first instance.

et al. (2000, 472), for instance, highlight O'Donnell's (1986) distinction between 'vertical' voice (talking to superiors above) and 'horizontal' voice (talking to friends, neighbours and family). 'Vertical' voice could be argued to be most costly, and this is especially the case in authoritarian regimes, while 'horizontal' would also come with potential costs in authoritarian regimes. Nonetheless, in the case of Kazakhstan while individuals might seek self-censorship when it comes to 'voice' among even family and friends, there is a culture of what is called 'kitchen politics', in that individuals feel comfortable voicing complaint about politics and policy in the confines of their kitchens, but outside in public such expression is contained. 'Voice' can also be conceived as being enacted either individually or in a collective (Dowding et al., 2000, 472). Such a framing has relevance to the phenomenon of opposition politics in Kazakhstan. The notion of individual 'voice' appeals to the very personalised nature of politics in the country. Even opposition politics tends to focus on a particular charismatic individual, and it is usually through that single individual through which opposition is channelled, framed and presented to the wider public. Because of the neopatrimonial political system, however, powerful individuals rely on a patronage network of clientelist support for the basis of their power (Ilkhamov, 2007; Isaacs, 2014; Ishiyama, 2002). Therefore, individuals often owe their loyalty to a particular powerful political figure whether they are considered in opposition or part of the regime. Nevertheless, that is not to say such powerful individuals do not evoke their voice and present it as collective voice (and thus somehow representing the majority) through the establishment of movements and especially political parties. Furthermore, the emergence of spontaneous grassroots-based opposition can also be divided between examples of collective and individual voice. As will be discussed in later chapters, there are numerous examples of stand-alone individual protest, even though they form part of a larger emerging political culture of protest.

Loyalty, Sanctions and Institutional Adaptation

The next central question is what influences the decision to enact any of these different forms of exit and/or voice? For Hirschman this is where the concept of loyalty emerged as an important factor in questions of public choice and he used it to explain why in certain contexts and organisations, such as family, tribe church and state, exit is practically unthinkable. Loyalty is a crucial intervening variable in neutralising 'within certain limits the tendency of the most quality-conscious customers or members to be the first to exit' (Hirschman, 1970, 79). While loyalty has been criticised as an 'ad-hoc equation filler' (Barry, 1974, 95), in the case of Central Asian authoritarianism loyalty does capture a 'real' social phenomenon, given the context of neopatrimonialism in the region (Ilkhamov, 2007; Isaacs, 2014).

Loyalty, therefore, emerges when 'a member with a considerable attachment to a product or organisation will often search for ways to make himself influential, especially when the organization moves in what he believes is the wrong direction' (Dowding et al., 2000, 475). This commitment to a particular product or organisation, what has been termed 'brand loyalty' or a 'psychological resistance to change', then must be understood in relation to the trade-off between the certainty of exit, to the uncertainty of potential improvements following voice within the organisation. Loyalty also exists in relation to an individual or collective's estimation of their ability to influence the organisation (Dowding et al., 2000, 475). Loyalty also has specific meaning in an authoritarian context. Loyalty could exist even with exit if the actor involved decides to exit with 'passive acceptance or even submissive silence' in relation to the status quo (Hoffmann, 2010, 57). It is the use of public voice with regard to the deficiencies of the regime and political system which are considered disloyal, and which could then face potential sanctions. While there has been some discussion on the extent to which there is an 'exit tax' (Dowding et al., 2000) on those who choose to leave an organisation, this perhaps has not been conceptualised enough in the literature. In an authoritarian setting the 'exit tax' can take the form or potential sanctions which then acts to condition individual and collective choice of remaining loyal by staying put and silent or exiting with or without public voice.

These sanctions (exit taxes) take can take four forms with the last being institutional adaptation (see Table 3.1). In the first instance there could be silence on the part of the regime to the expressing of a complaint or the exit. In an authoritarian context, while silence on the part of the regime may seem like no-sanction at all, it can be a strategy to ignore and de-legitimise such use of exit and voice by failing to acknowledge the existence of opposition. Secondly, sanctions can also take personal form in that they will be directed either individually at the person who has used

Table 3.1 Types of sanctions

	Type of sanction
0	Silence
1	Individual
2	Organisational
3	Institutional adaptation

their agency of exit or voice or that individual's family. This can include removal from public office, loss of business interests, tax inspection and even public trial and eventual imprisonment. At the level of non-elite grassroots opposition, individuals face the prospect of harassment, threats to physical security, arrest and imprisonment. Thirdly, sanctions can be applied at the organisational level to parties or movements associated with the individuals exiting from the regime and using public voice. This can include, for example, the banning or de-registering of such organisations from electoral competition. The final form of sanction is applied at the institutional or constitutional level as a form of institutional adaptation. Specific laws are designed, or amendments to the constitution are undertaken, which seek to deliberately hinder and make illegal the operations of such parties and movements. Institutional adaptation occurs when the opposition seems credible enough as a threat to regime stability. Thus, institutional adaptation is typically undertaken to strengthen the regime. However, as will be discussed further in this chapter and book, in the case of Kazakhstan institutional adaptation in response to opposition agency of exit and voice has the paradoxical effect of making the regime simultaneously both more stable and unstable.

An Exit, Voice, Loyalty Opposition-Regime Equilibrium and Mutually Constitutive Cycle of Regime-Opposition Relations

When exit, voice and loyalty is applied to the phenomenon of opposition politics in authoritarian political systems it requires complicating to take account of the different forms of exit and voice available to the various types of opposition actors (not just institutional forms of opposition). Here I outline an analytical framework which comprises four variations of exit, voice and loyalty, or more precisely the four nodal points on the regime-opposition equilibrium, which represent different contexts for the application of opposition agency (see Fig. 3.1). At each nodal point political opposition have a decision to make regarding whether to exit, use voice or remain loyal. The regime then responds with sanctions and/or institutional adaptation.

The first nodal point is for an actor to choose between using voice within the regime, by discussing with the leader (president) or group of elites regarding their concerns of declining democratic standards or regime deficiencies (this can include issues regarding the distribution of spoils), or whether to exit, or remain silent and loyal. This expression of voice is a form of 'vertical voice', in other words, speaking up to superiors (O'Donnell, 1986). Within the confines of the regime this is private voice, and it can represent a form of loyalty as it illustrates an attempt for a political actor to remain 'influential, especially when the organization moves in what he *[sic]* believes is the wrong direction' (Dowding et al., 2000, 475). The use of private voice could generally be low-cost in terms of potential sanctions. While there is a threat that individual sanctions could apply to the use of private voice, such as removal from an official

Nodal Point 1	Nodal Point 2
Voice within regime	Exit the regime (plus or minus voice)
Exit (plus or minus voice) the political system/country	Voice from outside the regime (non-oligarchic opposition voice)
Nodal Point 3	Nodal Point 4

Fig. 3.1 Four nodal point political opposition agency matrix in authoritarian systems

position or losing out in competition for economic resources, this is low-cost compared to the use of public voice outside the regime. However, we only become acutely aware of private voice when it fails and there is an exit from the regime.

At the second nodal point, disaffected elites whom having been unsuccessful in getting the regime to change course through private vertical voice can then choose to exit the regime. Barry has highlighted how there are at least two forms of exit in this instance. One is to decide to exit with 'passive acceptance or even submissive silence' (Hoffman, 2010, 57), and the other is to exit with voice and to 'campaign for improvements after leaving' (Barry, 1974, 92). The first represents the 'loyal' option and an attempt to avoid a high cost 'exit tax' (Dowding et al., 2000, 477). The choice of exit plus voice will usually solicit a response from the regime. This comes into two forms. Firstly, sanctions can be placed on the individual and/or the individual's organisation (such as a political party). This can include removal from public office, the barring from participating in an electoral competition for both parties and individuals and trial, prosecution and incarceration for various financial crimes. Secondly, institutional adaptation can be applied at a constitutional level. Specific laws are designed which deliberately hinder the operations of regime opponents, opposition parties and movements. This could include such constitutional revisions as changes to laws pertaining to political parties or elections. The choice for political opposition pertaining to exit, voice and loyalty is also conditioned by the experience of other members of the opposition who have already decided between exit and/or voice, and who may have been subject to individual and/or organisational sanctions, as well as being impacted in their ability to obtain political office by subsequent revisions to the institutional and constitutional architecture.

The third nodal point is where opposition decides to exit the political playing field altogether or the country. The choice is to exit in silence (the loyal option) or to continue to evoke public voice, but this time seeking international support. The decision is often calculated based on potential sanctions, especially the prospect of a trial and sentence in absentia, the risk of extradition back to the home country, danger to public organisations (such as the threat of de-registration or non-registration of a political party/movement or disbarment from electoral competition), and pressures on colleagues, friends and families. The decision to exit without voice involves a lower cost in terms of sanctions, although the threat of sanctions may continue to remain given the disruption caused to the regime.

The fourth nodal point concerns non-institutional opposition outside of the regime who use voice to make claims pertaining to policy as well as complaints regarding perceived deficiencies with the regime. This form of opposition can be non-elite, small or large social movements or trade unions, as well as individuals such as journalists, artists, NGO activists and human rights advocates. This type of opposition can generally emerge in what seems a spontaneous form without top-down direction in which self-organised grassroots groups, typically using social media, come together in response to specific policy issues or contingent events. Again, the regime will seek to put in place either individual or group sanctions and/or in some instances a form of institutional adaptation. In cases where the opposition to a specific policy emerges as a surprise to the regime—institutional adaptation can take the form of a recalibration of laws to illustrate the regime is responding to opposition complaints. For example, public commissions can be set up to account for policy concerns raised by opposition. In this way, the regime institutionally adapts to opposition demands which were triggered initially through public voice.

This final nodal point also leads us to something about the regime-opposition equilibrium which can appear when the threat from opposition is ambiguous and there is an absence of co-optation. In closed political systems the choice of exit or voice by political opposition functions as a signal regarding the diminishment of the quality of the government. Opposition agency in any of the four nodal points provides an opportunity for the regime to respond to the signal of weakness/instability to re-establish regime equilibrium.

Like in any authoritarian regime, opposition activity performs the role of feedback signal regarding weaknesses, policy gaps and governmental deficiencies. The feedback signal of exit, voice or loyalty allows the regime to correct its course, strengthen its position and re-shape the institutional architecture of the state to defend itself from further opposition claims (see Fig. 3.2). The problem in the case of Kazakhstan is that the credibility of the opposition is ambiguous. On the one hand, co-optation on the part of the regime is often absent, yet on the other hand the opposition still represents a serious enough threat that effort should go into sanctions and institutional adaptation to strengthen the regime. And in the case of Kazakhstan, observed in later chapters, this is what was responsible for the gradual decline and diminishment of formal institutional and oligarchic opposition from 1991 to 2013 and the consolidation of the regime around the personality of Nursultan Nazarbayev. However, at the same time, the concentration of power meant feedback signals pertaining to regime weaknesses and deficiencies diminished with time ultimately leaving the regime exposed to sporadic, unpredictable and more grassroots-based opposition, often catching the regime off guard. As will be discussed below, the Zhanaozen violence of 2011, land protests of 2016, youth activist election protests of 2019 and the 2022 *qandy qantar* protests are examples of this. This equilibrium is a self-reinforcing mutually constitutive cycle of reproduction. Opposition agency leads to sanctions and institutional adaptation which stabilises the regime which in turn leads to further opposition (but in different forms) and so on. It establishes a paradox of a constant process of regime stability and instability.

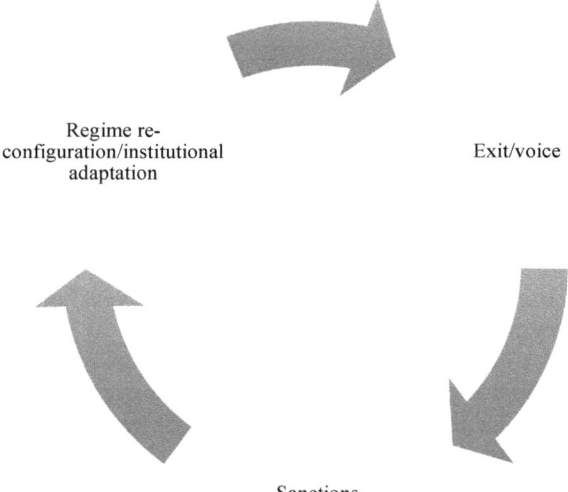

Fig. 3.2 Mutually constitutive cycle of regime and opposition in authoritarian settings

Conclusion

This chapter has developed an analytical framework to study the agency of political opposition in Kazakhstan using Hirschman's frame of exit, voice and loyalty. The framework takes account of the various ways in which exit, voice and loyalty can co-exist and the different options available for political opposition. These different choices are represented in the framework by the four nodal point matrix. Part II of this book will offer an empirical elaboration of the four nodal point matrix with reference to the agency and strategies available to political opposition in Kazakhstan. What the discussion reveals are the specific ways in which political opposition since the late 1990s has sought to navigate these nodal points of the exit and voice matrix and how the regime responded in terms of sanctions and institutional adaptation, thus eventually exposing them to further discontent. This is not meant to be an exhaustive account of political opposition in the country. There are other studies which detail the opposition in Kazakhstan more in-depth (Isaacs, 2011; Junisbai & Junisbai, 2005). Rather, the analysis in the following section provides exemplars of how the agency of political opposition can act to shape the regime-opposition equilibrium in a context where political opposition is not co-opted by the regime and the threat from the opposition is perceived as ambiguous.

References

Barry, B. (1974). Review article: Exit, voice, and loyalty. *British Journal of Political Science, 1*(4).

Brubaker, R. (1990). Frontier theses: Exit, voice and loyalty in East Germany. *Migration World, 18*(3/4), 12–17.

Dalmasso, E. (2018). Participation without representation: Moroccans abroad at a time of unstable authoritarian rule. *Globalizations, 15*(2), 198–214.

Dowding, K., John, P., Mergoupis, T., & Van Vugt, M. (2000). Exit, voice and loyalty: Analytic and empirical developments. *European Journal of Political Research, 37*(4), 469–495.

Hirschman, A. (1970). *Exit, voice and loyalty: Responses to decline in firms, organizations and states*. Harvard University Press.

Hirschman, A. (1993). Exit, voice, and the fate of the German democratic republic: An essay in conceptual history. *World Politics, 45*(2), 173–202.

Hoffmann, B. (2010). Bringing Hirschman back in: "Exit", "voice" and "loyalty" in the politics of transnational migration. *The Latin Americanist, 54*(2), 57–73.

Ilkhamov, A. (2007). Neopatrimonialism, interest groups and patronage networks: The impasses of the governance system in Uzbekistan. *Central Asian Survey, 26*(1), 65–84.

Isaacs, R. (2011). *Party system formation in Kazakhstan: Between formal and informal politics*. Routledge.

Isaacs, R. (2014). Neopatrimonialism and beyond! Re-assessing the formal and informal in Central Asian politics. *Contemporary Politics, 20*(2), 229–245.

Ishiyama, J. (2002). Neopatrimonialism and the prospects for democratization in the Central Asian Republics. In S. N. Cummings (Ed.), *Power and change in Central Asia* (pp. 42–58). Routledge.

Junisbai, B., & Junisbai, A. (2005). The democratic choice of Kazakhstan: A case study in economic liberalization, intra-elite cleavage and political opposition. *Demokratizatsiya: The Journal of Post-Soviet Democratization, 13*(2), 373–392.

Langston, J. (2002). Breaking out is hard to do: Exit, voice, and loyalty in Mexico's one-party hegemonic regime. *Latin American Politics and Society, 44*(3), 61–88.

Michaelsen, M. (2018). Exit and voice in a digital age: Iran's exiled activists and the authoritarian state. *Globalizations, 15*(2), 248–264.

Moses, W. (2005). Exit, vote and sovereignty: Migration, sates and globalization. *Review of International Political Economy, 12*(1), 53–77.

O'Donnell, G. (1986). On the fruitful convergences of Hirschman's exit, voice, and loyalty and shifting involvements: Reflections from the recent Argentine experience. In A. Foxley, M. S. McPherson, G. A. O'Donnell, and A. O. Hirschman (Eds.), *Development, democracy, and the art of trespassing: Essays in honour of Albert O. Hirschman* (pp. 251–252). University of Notre Dame Press.

Pfaff, S., & Kim, H. (2003). Exit-voice dynamics in collective action: An analysis of emigration and protest in the East German revolution. *American Journal of Sociology, 109*(2), 401–444.

Pirani, S. (2021, December 21). Who fired the shots? *The Ecologist*. Accessed online 24 January 2022. https://theecologist.org/2021/dec/16/who-fired-shots

PART II

Exit, Voice and Loyalty in Kazakhstan

CHAPTER 4

The Development of a Personalist-Authoritarianism Regime in Kazakhstan

Before we can discuss at length how the strategies and different forms of exit and voice have underpinned opposition agency in Kazakhstan, and contributed to regime-opposition relations, we must understand the context and dynamics within which contemporary forms of political opposition in Kazakhstan appeared. This chapter charts the trajectory of the relationship between regime and opposition in Kazakhstan from the Soviet period through to the first decade of independence in the country in the 1990s. In doing so, it provides a context for the development of the personalist authoritarian system which Nursultan Nazarbayev constructed in Kazakhstan.

The chapter firstly examines the nature of authority under soviet rule exploring the birth of the modern Kazakh state, the development of patrimonial communism and the emergence of early forms of opposition during the late Soviet period. Secondly, the chapter analyses the institutional crisis that the first president of Kazakhstan, Nursultan Nazarbayev, inherited with the collapse of the USSR and how it created a form of institutional opposition to his regime. Finally, the chapter then addresses how Nazarbayev curtailed this institutional opposition through a process of institutional adaptation (constitutional reform which rebalanced the power relations between the different branches of government). In doing

© The Author(s), under exclusive license to Springer Nature Switzerland AG 2022
R. Isaacs, *Political Opposition in Authoritarianism*, The Theories, Concepts and Practices of Democracy, https://doi.org/10.1007/978-3-031-06536-1_4

this, Nazarbayev began to consolidate a personalised form of authoritarian rule where legitimation became centred on personal attributes of the leader built upon a patronal form of politics in which resources and spoils are distributed to competing oligarchic elite groups. In such a context, with institutionalised opposition marginalised because of the regime's efforts of institutional adaptation, the main place for political opposition to emerge was from inside the regime itself in the shape of an oligarchic opposition, closely tied to key business and political elites. The chapter does not offer a full and detailed account of Kazakhstan's political history,[1] rather it only seeks to provide the context to the emergence of oligarchic opposition and their use of exit and voice as a form of agency which is the subject of the subsequent chapter.

The Birth of Modern Kazakhstan

The borders and state of modern-day Kazakhstan were constructed by Soviet officials in the 1920s and 1930s through national delimitation, a process through which the Soviet authorities sought to establish clearly defined territorial administrative units out of the former Russian Empire (Isaacs & Polese, 2015, 372; Sabol, 1995). There have been competing explanations for the purpose of national delimitation in the Central Asian region. Some scholars suggest it was part of a divide and rule strategy to advert the possibility of Pan-Turkic unity (Roy, 2000, 68). Others offer a revisionist account which points to the role of local elites in the process and views delimitation as part of a broader Soviet strategy of constructing and bringing together fragmented identities and establishing the USSR as a state of equal nations in the process (Edgar, 2004; Haugen, 2003, 234). National delimitation in Central Asia was a protracted process and it was not fully complete until 1936 when the Kazakh Autonomous Soviet Socialist Republic was finally elevated to the status of full Soviet republic. National delimitation is crucial to the story of authoritarianism in Kazakhstan, not just because the state of Kazakhstan as we understand it today would not exist without it, but also because present-day

---

[1] There are many existing published works which do this already, many of which are drawn upon in this chapter.

Kazakhstan's experience of statehood and its political-institutional architecture has been largely shaped by the Soviet experience, notably through patrimonial communism (see below).[2]

In the early Soviet period in Central Asia and Kazakhstan, this influence was channelled through the policy of *korenizatsiia* (nativisation) that sought to overcome the structural inequalities experienced by non-Russians (Liber, 1991, 16). This was to be achieved through the spread of mass literacy and education in native languages, the fostering of titular cultures and, perhaps most importantly for the development of authoritarianism in Kazakhstan, the co-optation of local elites into the Soviet apparatus (Ubiria, 2016, 149). Co-optation of local elites also went together with the destruction of political forces which opposed Soviet rule in the region. Notably, this included the Kazakh Alash party, an organisation established in the early 1900s which was led by a Russian-educated Kazakh intellectual elite who were dedicated to promoting the modernisation of Kazakh society through conceiving the peoples as a distinct culturally bounded national community (Kesici, 2017, 1135; Sdykov, 2012, 10). The Alash party was central to the formation of the Alash Orda, which was an autonomous Kazakh-dominated government established in late 1917, ostensibly with the backing of the White forces in the Russian civil war. By 1920, with the Bolsheviks defeating the White forces in Central Asia, the Alash Orda was disbanded, by which point members of the government had already acceded to Bolshevik rule and been riven by factional disputes (Amanzholova, 2009, 188; Ubiria, 2016, 77–78). Members of the Alash Orda either fled or found themselves under assault from the new Soviet authorities (Koigeldiev, 2007). Despite the nativisation of cadre through the policy of *korenizatsiia* and the quashing of nationalist opposition such as Alash, the newly Sovietised political elite in Kazakhstan faced a purge just as local elites faced in other parts of the USSR during the 1930s (Wheeler, 1964, 141–143). Thus, during its formative years, the modern Kazakh state was a tightly controlled political unit, where dissent and opposition was barely, if at all, tolerated. Such autocratic beginnings were to have a lasting imprint on the Kazakh state.

---

[2] This is not to deny that Kazakhs had some experience of proto statehood via the Kazakh Khanate which ebbed and flowed in various incarnations from the fifteenth until eighteenth centuries.

The Genesis of Personalist Authoritarianism in Soviet Kazakhstan

While the imprint of authoritarianism in Kazakhstan can be gauged through the lens of strict Soviet rule in the formative years of the Kazakh state's inception, it is important to also remember that as a new state, such authoritarian rule was channelled through key political institutions. For Kazakhstan, having never been an independent sovereign modern state before, Soviet political institutions were the only experience of political administration that the newly independent Kazakhstan had to go on. Nonetheless, it was the dynamics and development of political authority during the Brezhnev period, which was to have a lasting impact on the nature of authoritarian rule in Kazakhstan and thus consequently shaping the relationship between opposition and regime in the era of independence.

While the Stalinist period in Central Asia had been one of trauma (industrialisation, collectivisation and sedentarisation), direct rule from Moscow and intermittent purges of local elites accused of nationality-based localism, the post-Stalin period was one of greater stability (Critchlow, 1988, 144; Gleason, 1991, 615). The period of Leonid Brezhnev's leadership of the USSR brought with it a considerable degree of local elite stability in Central Asia. Whereas before there had been direct oversight from Moscow and frequent purges of local elites, under Brezhnev's policy of the 'stability of cadre', regional elites held long and stable tenures of rule. Consequently, from the late 1950s until the 1980s the First Secretaries of the Republican communist parties in Central Asia remained largely unchanged. In the case of Kazakhstan, Dinmukhamed Kunaev remained as First Secretary of the Communist Party of Kazakhstan from his appointment in 1960 until 1986 (apart from a two-year period between 1962 and 1964 when Khrushchev replaced him with Ismail Yusupov) (Critchlow, 1988). According to Yoram Gorlizki and Oleg Khlevniuk (2020, 258), Brezhnev's commitment to keeping local elites in power for such extended periods of time was partly out of necessity given the role they had played in ousting Khrushchev.

Nonetheless, there were significant consequences for the development of Kazakhstan's political system because of Brezhnev's decision to ensure stability of elites. Firstly, the long tenure allowed First Secretaries at the Republican level to entrench their personal authority over their respective republics. As James Critchlow (1988, 143) noted: the long tenure 'of the Central Asian First Secretaries enabled them to put their own personal stamp on the Republican machinery, as in a fiefdom, appointing their followers to senior posts at both *Oblast* (Regional) and *Raion* (District) level'. In Kazakhstan, this allowed Dinmukhamed Kunaev to create an expansive personal network of authority based on the principle of fealty (Gleason, 1991). While important positions within the Republic went to close family members, such as the appointment of Kunaev's brother, Askar, to the position of president of the Academy of Sciences, it also established a ruling principle in which resources and positions were distributed among close networks in exchange for loyalty to the individual ruler (Akkuly, 2011; Cummings, 2002). During his long tenure, Kunaev was generally perceived to be promoting the national interests of the Kazakhs while also not marginalising the considerable Slavic population in the republic. As Sally Cummings has argued, Kunaev 'built up an ethnic Kazakh, largely politico-administrative, cadre and helped sponsor the educational and cultural development of ethnic Kazakhs' (Cummings, 2005, 16). Secondly, and more importantly, this established what Critchlow (1988) defines as a form of patrimonial authority, or alternately patrimonial communism. A patrimonial communist regime 'relies on vertical chains of dependence between leaders in the state and party apparatus and their entourage, buttressed by extensive patronage and clientelist networks' (Kitschelt et al., 1999, 23). What this meant in practice is that political power was generally concentrated in the individual leader and/or their close elite circle, appointments and resources are distributed based on loyalty, nepotism and local favouritism to the leader, and this system of power intersected and interacted with Soviet institutional forms of governance, principally, the Communist Party (Critchlow, 1988, 143–145). This in effect established a 'two-level political culture' between the formal institutional politics of the state and party and an informal personalised political culture centred on the cult of personality (Roy, 2000, 85).

The consequence of patrimonial communism for Kazakhstan then and now is that it laid the foundation for the form of political system to emerge after the collapse of the Soviet Union, albeit stripped of any role for the Communist Party. During the Brezhnev era, Kunaev owed his position as First Secretary of the Kazakh Communist party out of fealty to Brezhnev, correspondingly Kunaev was able to engender stability to his rule in Kazakhstan by selecting personnel who were trusted for their loyalty to his leadership (Olcott, 1987, Chapter 10). Consequently, allegiance was to Kunaev, not to the Party or Moscow. It was in this context that Nursultan Nazarbayev (who would go on to be the first president of the Republic of Kazakhstan) climbed the ranks of the Kazakh Communist Party. Nazarbayev was a loyal protégé of Kunaev, and fealty paid off as Kunaev was instrumental in ensuring Nazarbayev was appointed as chairman of Kazakhstan's Council of Ministers, effectively the number two position in the Republic (Cummings, 2002). Nazarbayev's political schooling was in a system in which personalism and loyalty were fundamental, something he commented on himself in one of his early books. He notes that 'Brezhnev selected the party Central Committee leaders in the republics, and they in turn appointed the heads of the regional committees completely on the basis of personal loyalty' (Nazarbayev, 1992, 15). Patrimonial communism, and the way in which Brezhnev managed political relations among competing clientelist networks, serviced Nazarbayev in developing the appropriate bureaucratic skills and patronage necessary to rise to the top of Kazakhstan's party oligarchy (Olcott, 2002, 28).

Nazarbayev became leader of the Kazakh Republic in 1989, three years after Kunaev had been ousted as part of Gorbachev's effort to clean up the corruption which had become endemic in the system. The late USSR period of *glasnost* and *perestroika* sowed the seeds not only for the emergence of personalist authoritarian rule which Nazarbayev constructed in the post-Soviet period, which was premised upon the development of patrimonial communism of the Brezhnev and Kunaev period, but also for the mutually constitutive relationship between opposition and regime which defined Kazakhstan's political system after the USSR.

THE EMERGENCE OF OPPOSITION IN KAZAKHSTAN

The period of *glasnost* and *perestroika* (from 1986 to 1991) in the USSR witnessed the emergence of a more diverse and pluralistic political society. Across the different republics of the Soviet Union, new social movements, independent newspapers, political groupings and parties sprung up from 'every position on the political spectrum' and even 'wrested policy initiative away from Gorbachev' (Butterfield & Sedaitis, 1991, 1). In many Soviet republics, it was nationalist movements which tended to flourish, especially in the Baltics, and such organised groupings have been perceived to have played a significant role in the collapse of the USSR

(Beissinger, 2009; Lieven, 1993, 219–230). It was in Kazakhstan, in fact, in which one of the earliest manifestations of nationalist protest against heavy-handed Moscow control took place. *Zheltokan* (meaning December in Kazakh) was a student led-protest that occurred from the 16 to 18 December 1986 against the appointment of a Russian, Gennady Kolbin, as First Secretary of the Kazakh Communist Party in place of the long-serving Kunaev (Toguzbaev, 2011). Thousands of students participated in the initially peaceful protest until it was forcibly suppressed by Soviet military forces who used water cannons and shovels to beat the young people involved (Mukankyzy, 2014). A special commission of the Supreme Soviet of the Kazakh Soviet Socialist Republic found that 168 people died in the December events.[3]

Zheltoksan was just the beginning of the emergence of a form of opposition to Soviet power which was to appear in the late-USSR period in Kazakhstan. From 1986 to 1989 a plethora of social movements and discussion clubs appeared in the republic, mostly in the then capital, Alma-Ata, but also in all *oblasts* of the country (Ponomarev, 1991). These early groups were largely concerned with ecological issues, appearing initially in the Pavlodar region with the creation in 1987 of the Ecological and Public Opinion group—predominantly an educational organisation (Ponomarev, 1991, 61–62), and then the social-ecological organisation 'Initsiativa' in Alma-Ata (also established in 1987) which then merged with a series of other small ecological focused groups to form *Zelenogo Fronta* (Green Front) in 1988 (Zaslavskaya, 1994, 6–7). The most prominent of these groups was the Nevada-Semipalatinsk International Anti-nuclear and Ecological Movement established in 1989 and led by the poet Olzhas Suleimenov, which attracted thousands to protest in support of its aim to close the Soviet nuclear testing site in Semipalatinsk, a goal finally achieved in 1991 (Baizakova, 2021; Ponomarev, 1991, 43). There have been claims that the Soviet authorities (and even Nazarbayev) were behind the establishment of the organisation as a way to manage the developing pluralism in the country (Babak, 2005). As such, it was an early indication of the way in which political opposition could be managed by authorities through a policy of co-opting groups and movements that potentially posed a threat to the regime. It also illustrates that while such

---

[3] Zaklyuchenie komissi prezitsdiuma verkhovnogo soveta kazakhskoi SSR po okonchatel'noi otsenke dekabr'skikh sobytii 1986 goda v Alma-Ate – drygikh oblastyakh Kazakhstana. Alma-Ata: Pre prezitsdiuma verkhovnogo soveta kazakhskoi SSR, 1990.

environmental movements could ostensibly be viewed as non or apolitical, they were highly political because of the ways in which their agendas and programmes challenged the destructive effects of Soviet policies on the environment.

At the same time as Kazakhstan was witnessing the appearance of ecologically minded social movements, other more explicitly political grassroots movements were appearing in towns and cities across the country. Organisations such as the Alma-Ata Peoples Front, *Akikat* (Truth), *Zheltoksan* (an organisation set up by those involved in the events of December 1986) and Memorial, a group dedicated to rehabilitating victims of the Stalinist repressions, openly challenged the political and economic hegemony of communist elites (Buluktaev et al., 1998, 76). Notably the first 'opposition' parties appear also at this time after the Supreme Soviet of the USSR removed Article 6 from the 1977 constitution which had enshrined the leading role of the Communist Party. The political parties which appeared, among others, included The Alash Party, ostensibly a nationalist party, the Azat Movement which was dedicated to achieving full state sovereignty for Kazakhstan and the Social Democratic Party of Kazakhstan, a party of Russian-speaking urbanites (Zaslavskaya, 1994, 12–15). According to a former member of the Social Democratic Party, 'the opposition which appeared at this time could be characterised as anti-communist and democratic. These were dissidents and people who disliked Bolshevism and communism and who were Western oriented in the values they shared and in what they were thinking'.[4] This was an opposition which featured the intelligentsia, artists and writers, and who were largely without significant financial resources to support their opposition activities.[5] Full sovereignty and independence arrived for Kazakhstan on 16 December 1991, on the sixth anniversary of the *Zheltoksan* events. Kazakhstan was the last Soviet Republic to declare independence from the USSR.

---

[4] Author's interview with Yevgeni Zhovtis, Director of Kazakhstan International Bureau for Human Rights and the Rule of Law and member of the Social Democratic Party of Kazakhstan, 30 January 2007, Almaty, Kazakhstan.

[5] Author's interview with Sergei Duvanov, independent journalist and original member of the Social Democratic Party of Kazakhstan, 28 November 2006.

Institutional Crisis and Adaptation

Once the position of president had been created across Soviet republics in 1990, Nazarbayev was elected by the Supreme Soviet of Kazakhstan as the country's first president. However, newfound independence in 1991 brought with it considerable challenges. Alongside the obvious nation-building, state-building and economic challenges, Nazarbayev faced political challenges in terms of regime-building. The multitude of political opposition which emerged during the late-Soviet period represented numerous potential threats to the stability of his nascent regime. Likewise, the unstable balance of powers between the institutions of the state also represented a threat. Initially most of these potential threats were addressed through institutional adaptation which in turn paved the way for the consolidation of Nazarbayev's personalist authoritarian regime. While threats to Nazarbayev's position could be understood across several dimensions (not least the internal threat of ethnic, religious or nationalist mobilisation and the external threat of Russian revanchism), here I will focus principally on the institutional dimension pertaining to threats to his rule. This concerns the configuration of powers between the executive and legislature within the new Kazakhstani state and the emergence of an institutional opposition to his rule and policy programme.

The first constitution of Kazakhstan was adopted on 28 January 1993 and was passed in the Supreme Soviet with only three abstentions. However, for deputies involved in the discussion on the constitution at the time, 'it was clear that the 1993 constitution did not suit the president and the executive' (Mamashuly, 2020). The 1993 constitution placed significant checks on the power of the executive by ensuring that the president had to report to the legislature and that he would not be able to dissolve parliament at will. As John Anderson noted, the constitution provided the parliament with 'a wide range of formal rights including the right to approve the budget, amend the constitution and elect the constitutional court' (Anderson, 1997, 307). The Supreme Soviet, which had only been established in April 1990 as part of Gorbachev's reforms, had emerged as a powerful institutional force as 'the original creator of laws in the state' (Abdil'din, 1993, 4). In less than four years of work the parliament had adopted 265 laws, including some of the most significant legislative acts in Kazakhstan's history (Zimanov, 2011).[6] The legislature also consisted of deputies who still held interests in former communist organisations and state enterprises, thus representing a form of institutional opposition to Nazarbayev's intended economic reform programme (Gleason, 1997; Olcott, 2002, 101). This institutional form of opposition could be largely observed in the Socialist Party of Kazakhstan (a reform-minded successor organisation to the Communist Party, established in 1992), the Communist Party of Kazakhstan (those ideologically unrepentant deputies and elites who saw themselves as the 'real' successors to the old Communist Party), and the Party of Peoples Congress of Kazakhstan led by Olzhas Suleimenov established in October 1991 (which developed out of the Nevada-Semipalatinsk movement). In response to the emergence of opposition parties, the president established a new pro-government political party, the Union of Peoples Unity of Kazakhstan (SNEK).

The parliamentary election of 7 March 1994 for the Supreme Kenges, the new 177 seat legislative body established in the 1993 constitution, did little to ease the institutional friction. Despite SNEK winning the largest number of seats (30) the legislature remained a bastion of opposition. The first convocation of a professional parliament in Kazakhstan undertook a series of actions which undermined Nazarbayev and the government. This included not electing the president's candidate for parliamentary speaker, passing a vote of no-confidence in the government, overriding the presidential veto on two bills, a continued resistance to the government's economic reform programme and using the legislative chamber to publicly criticise Nazarbayev's leadership (Olcott, 1997, 113). With this continued institutional instability and threat to his authority, Nazarbayev responded by seeking to foreclose the opposition through institutional adaptation which sought to readdress the constitutional balance of power. This was achieved firstly, through getting the constitutional court to annul the election and dissolve the parliament through a constitutional technicality from a single filed compliant from one candidate in one district in the election (for more on this see Zimanov, 2011). Secondly, in the interregnum eight-month period before a new election was held for the

---

[6] This included the creation of the post of president (24 April 1990), the Declaration on the State Sovereignty of the Kazakh SSR (25 October 1990), the Law on State Independence of the Republic of Kazakhstan (16 December 1991) and the new Constitution (28 January 1993) (Aitkhozhin & Buluktaev, 2003).

legislature, the executive branch devised a new constitution (without consultation) which invested more powers in the presidency (including the power to dissolve parliament at will and the power of appointment of the cabinet, senior members of the judiciary and other government positions) and which was subsequently passed by referendum (Mamashuly, 2020). The opportunity was also used to establish a new institutional body, the Assembly of Peoples of Kazakhstan (APK), which was appointed by the president and meant to represent the many nationalities living in Kazakhstan. Finally, the period without the legislature was used to push through the president's economic reform agenda by presidential decree. 134 presidential decrees were issued during the eight months, many relating to privatisation of banking activities, gas, tax, land code, elections, parliament and the budget for 1996 (Burkhanov et al., 2006, 84–85). According to Zauresh Batalova, a former senator, the annulling of the 1993 constitution and Nazarbayev's move to rule through decree amounted to a 'constitutional coup'.[7]

The election of the new slimed down legislature[8] in December 1995, under the conditions of the revised constitution, did ease the institutional oppositional pressure on the president and marginalised opposition to his rule and programme. Opposition representation in the new convocation was reduced to 7–9% of deputies (Zhani, 2007). A slate of new smaller pro-government parties that had been backed by the executive alongside Nazarbayev's Party of Peoples Unity of Kazakhstan made up the bulk of party representation in parliament. The People's Congress of Kazakhstan was reduced to a single seat, and its leader, Olzas Suleimenov chose exit, loyalty and co-optation by accepting Nazarbayev's offer of a diplomatic post as Kazakhstan's Ambassador to Italy. The largest oppositional representation came in the form of the Communist Party (2 seats), led by the former speaker of parliament Serikbolsyn Abdil'din. Abdil'din claimed that the Communist Party had received a larger percentage of the vote and should have been awarded more seats but that the election result had been falsified.[9]

---

[7] Author's interview with Zauresh Batalova, 25 April 2019, Nur-Sultan, Kazakhstan.

[8] The new legislature, the *Mazhilis* (parliament), was reduced to just 67 seats, from the previous 177, but an upper chamber senate was also established consisting of 40 members who were indirectly elected by local bodies and 7 directly appointed by the president.

[9] Author's interview with Serikbolysn Abdil'din, 30 January 2007, Almaty, Kazakhstan.

While Nazarbayev's consolidation of power can be observed as the beginning of the foreclosing of institutional opposition, attempts were also made to circumscribe the plethora of public associations and political parties which had emerged in the late Soviet and early post-Soviet period. Formal laws on political parties and public associations were adopted in 1996. While neither were expressly authoritarian, they did begin the process of placing constraints on the ability of groups to register and function compared to the ease at which organisations could register and operate until this point. For example, the 1996 Law on Political Parties restricted the establishment of political parties to no less than ten citizens convoking a constituent congress with no less than 3000 members in at least half the *Oblasts* of the country.[10] As discussed in the following chapter, the Law on Political Parties became an important tool in the president's arsenal of sanctions in reaction to the emergence of opposition voice. The post-95 constitution period also saw Nazarbayev consolidate his control of the bureaucracy by cutting back on staff numbers in government ministries and departments (Cummings, 2005). This had the benefit of also removing the cabinet and ministry system of being a potential area of political contestation (Olcott, 2002, 114). What was occurring to observers at the time was that Nazarbayev was establishing a strong personalist form of presidential authority (Zimanov, 2011).

THE DEVELOPMENT OF A PERSONALIST AUTHORITARIAN REGIME IN KAZAKHSTAN

The institutional conflict between the executive and the legislature that had defined the early years of Kazakhstan's independence ultimately began the foreclosing of opposition in the country. Institutional parliamentary opposition was now circumscribed by the changes put into effect after the introduction of the 1995 constitution. What this allowed for was the development of political authority centred on the personality of Nazarbayev. As the former leader of the Communist Party of Kazakhstan noted, 'all state bodies work for one person and therefore no one can influence him (Nazarbayev) besides his family and clan...power is taken away from the people and they (the regime) are strengthening

---

[10] Zakon Respubliki Kazakhstan O politicheskikh partikh, 1996, in I. O. Buluktaev, C. A. D'yachenko and L. I. Karmazina, *Politicheskie Partii Kazakhstana Spravochnik 1998* (Almaty: IPK, 1998).

the cult of the president'.[11] Thus, what developed in Kazakhstan was not dissimilar to patterns of authority in other former Soviet states. Henry Hale has termed the intersection between formal executive power and informal personal authority as patronal presidentialism. Under a patronal presidential regime, directly elected executive authority has considerable powers invested in it compared to other institutional bodies, but at the same time politics is organised around 'personalised exchange of concrete rewards and punishments through chains of actual acquaintance, and not primarily around abstract, impersonal principles such as ideological belief or categorizations' (Hale, 2014, 9–10). In other words, in the case of the presidency of Nursultan Nazarbayev, while the president is ostensibly directly elected (through elections which are often described by international monitors as flawed) and possesses extensive executive powers compared to the legislature and judiciary, what matters more in terms of the operation of political decision-making is informal personal authority. Nazarbayev created a political system whereby elite personnel positions were appointed directly by him and, therefore, elites were aware that they served the president and his personal interests (Masanov, 2000). According to Nurbolat Masanov (2000) this equated to a 'protectorship-client system gravitating to oligarchic forms with a supreme patron on top of the power pyramid'. The president appoints the most senior governing (at national and local levels) elites, who in turn appoint their people into important positions under them, who then can appoint officials under their charge and so on. Each level owes loyalty to the above and Nazarbayev was at the top overseeing it all. Nazarbayev's powers of appointment were vast and wide, and as the human rights campaigning Sergei Duvanov argued such 'political positions are not based on rational lines of divisions but 'depend on the will of one man'.[12] There are shades of patrimonial communism in these series of dyadic interconnected patron–client relations, as these relationships play an important role in the exchange of resources, information and services (Masanov, 2000).

But what also developed during this period in Kazakhstan were more informal forms of oligarchic power which existed outside of official state positions. Like the privatisation policy in Russia, the Kazakhstani government initiated a form of shock therapy which saw major industrial

---

[11] Author's interview with Serikbolsyn Abdil'din.
[12] Author's interview with Sergei Duvanov.

and service sectors of the economy sold off through voucher schemes via specifically set up Investment Privatisation Funds with the aim that vouchers would be available to a wide swath of the population (Pomfret, 2005). Again, much like in Russia, the opposite happened as shares in major enterprises (e.g., oil, gas and banking sectors) were consolidated in just a few of the Investment Privatisation Funds. Emerging from this were a series of very wealthy oligarchic groups—some of which were family members of the president. These oligarchic groups were called *gruppy vliyaniya* (groups of influence) because from the mid to late 1990s onwards they struggled between each other over two types of resources (1) influence over the president and his decision-making, especially as it came to policies which concerned their business interests and (2) access to the distribution of resources that were made available in Kazakhstan's shift to a market economy (Eurasian Centre of Political Research and Agency for Social Technologies, 2005).[13] On this basis, these groups owed a personal loyalty to Nazarbayev because he was the 'reason they have all their wealth'.[14] Loyalty to the president delivered access to resources and further stakes in the privatising economy (Grosin, 2005). Nazarbayev, therefore, played the key role as arbitrator of the struggles between these different *gruppy vliyaniya* over access to resources. A further important component which is essential to understanding the trigger for the exit of some sections of these oligarchic groups from the confines of the Nazarbayev regime, and which is the central subject of the subsequent chapter, is that in the late 1990s, Nazarbayev began giving considerable preference to family members and very close associates in these conflicts over access to resources. One notable and now famous example was that of his son-in-law, Rakhat Aliyev, married to his eldest daughter Dariga Nazarbayev, who was appointed as head of the tax police (Khulupin, 2000).[15]

---

[13] A breakdown of these different groups is not necessary here. They will appear empirically in the subsequent chapter. The nature of these groups is that overtime they fluctuate in terms of their position of strength. Since the late 1990s some of these groups have disappeared or re-constituted themselves in different forms. A breakdown of some of the most influential groups from the late 1990s until the mid 2000s can be found in Isaacs (2011, Chapter 3).

[14] Author's interview with Yevgenni Zhovtis.

[15] More details on some of the family and close associate appointments made by Nazarbayev during this period can be found in Amrekulov (2000).

Concluding Remarks

By the late 1990s Nursultan Nazarbayev had consolidated his authority in Kazakhstan. This had been achieved principally by marginalising institutional opposition in the legislature by engineering its dissolution and re-writing the constitution to give himself greater executive power. At the same time, an authoritarian regime had developed where personal loyalty to the president was a central characteristic, patron–client relations were endemic, the power of appointment a fundamental dynamic, and where oligarchic groups rich off the back of the privatisation process competed for influence over the president. Therefore, with limited institutional opposition within the parliament, political opposition in Kazakhstan, and the agency of political opposition, would emerge within this oligarchic elite. It would be the 'voice' and 'exit' of some of these *gruppy vliyaniya* which would come to shape the dynamics of regime-opposition relations in Kazakhstan from the late 1990s onwards.

References

Abdil'din, S. (1993). *Stanovlenie Parlamentarizma v Kazakhstane*. Sekretariat Soveta MPA.

Aitkhozhin, K., & Buluktaev, Y. (2003). *Rol' Parlamenta v sisteme gosudarstvennoi vlasti*. Tsentr Analiza Obshchestvennykh Problem.

Akkuly, S. (2011, April 9). Zakat Askara Kunaeva predveshal skoryi konets Kunavea-starshego. *Radio Azattyk*. Accessed online 16 Dec 2021. https://rus.azattyq.org/a/askar_kunaev_december_riot_kazakhstan_/3551546.html

Amanzholova, D. (2009). *Na Izlome. Alash v ethnopoliticheskoi istorii Kazakhstana*. Izdatel'skii dom 'Taimas'.

Amrekulov, N. (2000). Zhuzy v sotsialno-politicheskoi zhizni Kazakhstana. *Tsentral'naia Aziia i Kavkaz, 3*(9), 131–146.

Anderson, J. (1997). Constitutional development in Central Asia. *Central Asian Survey, 16*(3), 301–320.

Babak, V. (2005). Kazakhstan: How its multiparty system came into being. *Central Asia and the Caucasus, 32*(2), 1–14.

Baizakova, G. (2021, February 28). 32 goda nazad voznikloa zactavivshee zamolchat yadernyi polygon dvizhenie Nevada-Semei'. *Kazinform*. Accessed online 18 Dec 2021. https://www.inform.kz/ru/32-goda-nazad-vozniklo-zastavivshee-zamolchat-yadernyy-poligon-dvizhenie-nevada-semey_a3758590

Beissinger, M. (2009). Nationalism and the collapse of the Soviet Union. *Contemporary European History, 18*(3), 331–347.

Buluktaev, Y. O., D'yachenko, C. A., & Karmazina, L. I. (1998). *Politicheskie Partii Kazakhstana Spravochnik 1998*. IPK.

Burkhanov, K., Sultanov, B., & Ayagan, A. (2006). *Sovremennaia Politicheskaia Istoriia Kazakhstana*. Institut Istorii i etnologii im. Ch. Ch. Valikhanova.

Butterfield, J., & Sedaitis, J. (1991). The emergence of social movements in the Soviet Union. In J. Sedaitis & J. Butterfield (Eds.), *Perestroika from below social movements in the Soviet Union* (pp. 1–12). Westview Press.

Collins, K. (2006). *Clan politics and regime transition in Central Asia*. Cambridge University Press.

Critchlow, J. (1988). Corruption Nationalism and the Native Elites in Soviet Central Asia. *The Journal of Communist Studies, 4*(2), 143–161.

Cummings, S. N. (2002). An uneasy relationship—Power and authority in the Nazarbayev regime. In S. N. Cummings (Ed.), *Power and change in Central Asia* (pp. 59–73). Routledge.

Cummings, S. N. (2005). *Kazakhstan power and elite*. I.B. Tauris.

Edgar, A. (2004). *Tribal nation: The making of Soviet Turkmenistan*. Princeton University Press.

Eurasian Centre of Political Research and the Agency for Social Technologies. (2005). *Gruppy vliyaniia vo vlastno-policheskoi sisteme Respubliki Kazakhstan*. Accessed 21 Dec. http://www.matritca.kz/news/34004-vspomnit-vse-gruppy-vliyaniya-vo-vlastno-politicheskoy-sisteme-respubliki-kazahstan-god-2005-y.html

Gleason, G. (1991). Fealty and loyalty: Informal authority structures in Soviet Asia. *Soviet Studies, 43*(4), 613–628.

Gleason, G. (1997). *The Central Asian states: Discovering independence*. Westview Press.

Gorlizki, Y., & Khlevniuk, O. (2020). *Substate dictatorship: Networks, loyalty, and institutional change in the Soviet Union*. Yale University Press.

Grosin, A. (2005). *Kto est kto v sovremenom Kazakhstane. Zanimatel'no – o klanovykh gruppirovkakh*. Instituta Stran SNG.

Hale, H. (2014). *Patronal politics: Eurasian regime dynamics in comparative perspective*. Cambridge University Press.

Haugen, A. (2003). *The establishment of national republics in Soviet Central Asia*. Palgrave Macmillan.

Isaacs, R. (2011). *Party system formation in Kazakhstan: Between formal and informal politics*. Routledge.

Isaacs, R., & Polese, A. (2015). Between "imagined" and "real" nation-building: Identities and nationhood in post-Soviet Central Asia. *Nationalities Papers, 43*(3), 371–382.

Kesici, O. (2017). The Alash movement and the question of Kazakh ethnicity. *Nationalities Papers, 45*(6), 1135–1149.

Khulupin, V. N. (2000, April 22). *Kazakhstanskaia Politicheskaia elita mezhdu modernizatsiei i traibalizom*. Report to the Second All-Russian Congress of Political Scientists, Moscow MGIMO. Accessed 21 Dec 2021. https://www.neweurasia.info/archive/2000/top5/05_26_26.051.htm

Kitschelt, H., Mansfeldova, Z., Markowski, R., & Tóka, G. (1999). *Postcommunist party systems: Competition, representation, and inter-party cooperation*. Cambridge University Press.

Koigeldiev, M. (2007). The Alash movement and the Soviet government: A difference of positions. In U. Tomohiko (Ed.), *Empire, Islam, and politics in Central Eurasia*. Slavic Research Centre, Hokkaido University.

Liber, G. (1991). Korenizatsiia: Restructuring Soviet nationality policy in the 1920s. *Ethnic and Racial Studies, 14*(1), 15–23.

Lieven, A. (1993). *The Baltic revolution: Estonia, Latvia, Lithuania and the path to independence*. Yale University Press.

Mamashuly, A. (2020, January 28). Konstitutsiya kotoraya ne ustroila Nazarbayeva. Osnovnoi zakon 1993 goda. *Radio Azattyk*. Accessed 19 Dec 2021. https://rus.azattyq.org/a/kazakhstan-constitution-1993-parliament-and-presidential-powers/30401326.html

Masanov, N. (2000). Political elite in Kazakhstan: The changes of Kazakhstani political elite during the period of sovereignty. *International Eurasian Institute for Economic and Political Research*. Almaty. Accessed 16 Apr 2009. http://iicas.org/english/publ_22_11_00.htm

Mukankyzy, M. (2014, April 6). Dekabr'skie sobytiya v uchebnikakh istorii. *Radio Azattyk*. Accessed 17 Dec 2021. https://rus.azattyq.org/a/kazakhstan-december-events-in-schoolbooks/25221330.html

Nazarbayev, N. (1992). *Without right and left*. Class Publishing.

Olcott, M. (1987). *The Kazakhs*. Hoover Institution Press.

Olcott, M. (1997). Nursultan Nazarbayev as a strong president. In R. Taras (Ed.), *Post-communist presidents*. Cambridge University Press.

Olcott, M. (2002). *Kazakhstan unfulfilled promise*. Brookings Institution Press.

Pomfret, R. (2005). Kazakhstan's economy since independence: Does the oil boom offer a second chance for sustainable development? *Europe-Asia Studies, 57*(6), 859–876.

Ponomarev, V. A. (1991). *Obshchestvennye organizatsii v Kazakhstane i Kyrgyzstane (1987–1991)*. Glagol.

Roy, O. (2000). *The New Central Asia: The creation of nations*. I.B. Tauris.

Sabol, S. (1995). The creation of Soviet Central Asia: The 1924 national delimitation. *Central Asian Survey, 14*(2), 225–241.

Sdykov, M. (2012). *Istoriiya Zapadnogo otdelniya Alash-Ordy*. Zapadno-Kazakhstanskii oblastnoi tsentr istorii i arkheologii.

Toguzbaev, K. (2011, July 7). Kolbina pokazali kazakhskim rukovoditelyam eshche letom 1986 goda. *Radio Azattyk.* Accessed 17 Dec 2021. https://rus.azattyq.org/a/zakash_kamalidenov_1986_book_/24255023.html

Ubiria, G. (2016). *Soviet nation-building in Central Asia: The making of the Kazakh and Uzbek Nations.* Routledge.

Wheeler, G. (1964). *The modern history of Soviet Central Asia.* Weidenfield and Nicolson.

Zaslavskaya, M. B. (1994). *Politicheskie partii i obshchestvennye ob'edineniya Kazakhstana na sovermennom etape razvitiia.* KISI.

Zhani, F. (2007, August 19). Kazakhstan Kontr-evoliotsiia parlamenta, ili Kratkaia istoriia izgnaniia oppozitsii. *Fergana.ru.* Accessed 20 Dec 2021. http://www.ferghana.ru/article.php?id=5295

Zimanov, S. (2011). *Parlament Kazakhstana v trudnye gody provozglasheniya nezavisimosti.* Alash baspasy.

CHAPTER 5

Exit, Voice and Loyalty—Opposition Strategies and Choice from Above in Kazakhstan, 1998–2011

In the previous chapter, we saw that the consolidation of a personalist authoritarian regime in Kazakhstan via the marginalisation of institutional opposition led to the foreclosure of the political space. In the 1990s Nursultan Nazarbayev constructed a regime where oligarchic groups competed for influence over the president and over access to economic resources. This chapter explores how this oligarchic opposition emerged from the regime and how their agency through exit and voice contributed to regime stability and instability. Using the four-nodal point political opposition agency matrix pertaining to exit and voice outlined in Chapter 2, this chapter provides an account of how oligarchic opposition in Kazakhstan moved through the different stages of exit and voice, while the regime responded with sanctions and institutional adaptation. As a reminder, the four-nodal points of opposition agency as forms of exit and voice are: voice inside the regime (private voice), exit the regime (either with or without public voice), exit the political system/country (either with or without public voice) and non-oligarchic voice outside the regime. What the analysis reveals is how the opposition and regime in Kazakhstan were locked in a mutually constituted relationship—as opposition agency via exit and voice was then countered by sanctions and institutional adaptation which then conditioned further agency from the opposition.

© The Author(s), under exclusive license to Springer Nature Switzerland AG 2022
R. Isaacs, *Political Opposition in Authoritarianism*, The Theories, Concepts and Practices of Democracy, https://doi.org/10.1007/978-3-031-06536-1_5

This chapter will focus on the first three of these nodal points of opposition agency (non-oligarchic voice outside the regime will be the subject of the next chapter). In doing so, the chapter details how at the first nodal point we can identify three examples of voice inside the regime beginning in 1998 with former Prime Minister Akezhan Kazhegeldin, in 2001 with the emergence of the movement *Demokraticheskii Vybor Kazakhstana* (Democratic Choice of Kazakhstan [DVK]), and in 2004 with Zamanbek Nurkadilov, a former Mayor of Almaty. In each case, voice was raised within the confines of the regime about the quality of democratic governance and preference given to the president's family in the sale of former state-owned enterprises. The Nazarbayev regime failed to see this opposition as a credible threat and did not offer co-optation in exchange for support. Instead, these oligarchic opposition elites moved towards the second nodal point of exiting the regime while using public voice against Nazarbayev and the political system he established. This led to a response on behalf of the regime which included personal sanctions against the individuals involved including tax fraud investigations, arrests, prosecution and harassment and institutional adaptation featuring changes to the law on political parties, law on elections and the constitution which sought to marginalise and penalise the oligarchic opposition. The response from the regime represents a paradox because on the one hand the regime saw the threat of the post-1998 opposition as credible enough to go to considerable lengths to marginalise and push them out of the political process, but also as not credible enough for regime co-optation.

The tough response from the regime in terms of sanctions and institutional adaptation pushed the opposition to the third nodal point of exiting the political system and in some instances the country altogether. The chapter details the experiences of leading figures from Kazakhstan's oligarchic opposition including: Akezhan Kazhegeldin, Galyman Zhakiyanov, Mukhtar Ablyazov, Bolat Abilov, among many others who either left the political system or country and remained silent given the toll individual sanctions had taken on their careers and lives.

What the chapter argues is that while in the short-term sanctions and institutional adaptation insulated the regime from further threats to its stability, at the same time such a regime response closed off the feedback signal opposition agency via exit and voice provided. The regime could previously ascertain from opposition voice any defects with policy or regime strategy. Opposition voice as a feedback signal was then used by the regime to correct its course and stabilise its position. Once this feedback signal had been removed by the early 2010s the regime was left vulnerable to unpredictable voice from outside the oligarchic opposition.

The chapter is organised into three sections, each representing one of the three specific nodal points. We begin with a discussion on the emergence of voice within the regime.

Exit, Voice, Loyalty and Sanctions in Kazakhstan

Nodal Point 1: Voice Inside the Regime

Observing and analysing the use of voice inside an authoritarian regime is difficult because of the opaque nature of such regimes. We may only become aware of internal regime voice once those expressing their concerns go public. As noted above, since 1998 it has been possible to observe three instances of the attempted use of voice from within the confines of the Nazarbayev regime. Two of these are individual cases: the former Prime Minister Akezhan Kazhegeldin in 1998; and Chairman of the Emergency Situations Committee, Zamanbek Nurkadilov in 2004; and the other is an organisational form of internal voice manifested by the establishment in 2001 of DVK, a group of leading members of the government and prominent businessmen who sought to put pressure on Nazarbayev regarding political reform in the country. Available information suggests that in all three cases there were private appeals to the president with regard to some perceived deficiency within the political system or in relation to the balance of elite interests in Kazakhstan.

With Kazhegeldin in 1998, and DVK in 2001, the major concern which led to the use of private voice was the behaviour of the president's then son-in-law Rakhat Aliyev. Aliyev was perceived to be trying to accrue a large business portfolio and was, according to one of the leaders of DVK, 'openly against some of the representatives of Kazakhstani business'.[1] In the case of Kazhegeldin, it was alleged that the ex-Prime Minister had approached the president and demanded 'if you fail to take actions to reign in your son-in-law I will resign'.[2] Since 1997, Rakhat

---

[1] Author's interview with Galymzhan Zhakiyanov ex-Akim of Semipalatinsk and Pavlodar Oblasts, January 10, 2007, Almaty, Kazakhstan.

[2] Author's interview Amirzhan Kosanov, former member of the Republican Peoples Party of Kazakhstan & OSDP, 25 February 2016, Almaty, Kazakhstan.

Aliyev, who was Head of the Tax Police, had created a secret department which monitored the activities of the most successful businesses in Kazakhstan. He was perceived to have used his position to arbitrarily and illegally take-over businesses in the country by raiding potential competitors' interests (Eurasian Transition Group, 2009; Junisbai, 2010, 247–249).[3] While the emergence of DVK was arguably a consequence of conflict between competing elite interests, it was also representative of a dissatisfaction with the slow pace of reform and the 'clash between what the president was saying and what these "young reformers" believed the president was doing in reality'.[4] The preference given to Aliyev in the selling off of former state enterprises, alongside the perceived lack of democratic reform in the country, led to several members of the government, and private business, voicing their concern privately to Nazarbayev. Among them included: Mukhtar Ablyazov, ex-Energy Minister, Galymzhan Zhakiyanov, *Akim* (governor) of Pavlodar Oblast, Bolat Abilov, a Deputy of the *Mazhilis* (parliament) and a member of the Political Council of the president's party *Otan* (Fatherland)[5] and Oraz Zhandosov, Deputy Prime Minister. This form of informal lobbying is evocative of the personalist nature of the regime based on loyalty and patronage in which 'the role of the president is that of an arbitrator trying to balance these different elite interests'.[6] It is also evidence of the 'closed politics inside the elite'[7] and the way in which elites express dissatisfaction with the status quo internal to the regime.

Comparable internal regime voice appears in the case of Zamanbek Nurkadilov. When going public with criticisms about the corruption he believed to be inherent to the Nazarbayev regime, Nurkadilov detailed the private conversations he held with the president:

> Once we (Nurkadilov and Nazarbayev) were very amicable, we shared plans for the future, talked much, argued, and were reconciled. We swore and

---

[3] Author's interview with anonymous member of AK Zhol Party, 18 January 2007, Almaty, Kazakhstan.

[4] Author's interview Vladimir Kozlov, former Leader of DVK Alga, 9 January 2007, Almaty, Kazakhstan.

[5] Otan was established by the authorities by a merger of a series of smaller pro-presidential parties with the Peoples Unity of Kazakhstan.

[6] Author's interview with Yevgeni Zhovtis.

[7] Author's interview with Yevgeni Zhovtis.

literally used strong language and expressions. Then the meetings became rarer. For the last three years we met four times for two-to three hours and spoke frankly, not about families and friendship, but about the future of Kazakhstan. I received too much information from ordinary people regarding their problems and troubles and I told him about it…I thought that he understood all my comments, but I was mistaken… (Alzhanov, 2004)

What Nurkadilov's statement neatly exemplifies is that we are only aware of private voice once dissatisfied elite go public with their complaints, and hence once they have exited the confines of the regime. Personal dissatisfaction, therefore, transforms into political dissatisfaction.[8] After making his criticisms public Nurkadilov was fired from his position as Emergencies Minister.

Nodal Point 2: Exit Regime with Voice

In the case of Kazakhstan, if the use of voice inside the regime ultimately fails (the president did not rein in Aliyev's activities or push for the political reform requested by Kazhegeldin and the DVK), the strategic choice available to dissatisfied political elites is to go public with their complaints. Going public and voicing grievances does not necessarily prefigure exit from the regime. Nonetheless, the act of overtly voicing discontent with the political system, and the balancing of elites which underpins power, implies either that the individual or group of elites concerned will leave their positions and exit the regime, or will face being dismissed.

Kazhegeldin originally stood down as Prime Minister in October 1997, ostensibly on grounds of poor health (Fuller, 1999). He continued to serve as an advisor to the president, while also setting up The Union of Industrialists and Entrepreneurs of Kazakhstan.[9] Prior to his resignation as Prime Minister, Kazhegeldin had also incited the wrath of the Chairman of the National Security Committee of Kazakhstan (KNB), Alnur Musayev—a close associate of Rakhat Aliyev—after he had given an interview where he made allegations concerning money laundering within the KNB dating back to the end of the Soviet period (Shurga, 1999). Kazhegeldin made his criticisms of the political system in Kazakhstan

---

[8] Author's interview Amirzhan Kosanov.
[9] Author's interview Amirzhan Kosanov.

public in the summer of 1998 with the publication of his book *Kazakhstan: The Right to Choose*. While not formally criticising Nazarbayev, the text of Kazhegeldin's book critiqued the economic and political stagnation in the country and it was clear whom this broadside was directed at. Kazhegeldin states in the book 'there are no direct parliamentary social controls on executive power. The government's clumsy meddling in the economy causes corruption to flourish, and the legal system is extremely weak' (Kazhegeldin, 1998a).

Kazhegeldin announced his intention to stand in the snap presidential election of January 1999 and subsequently sharpened his censure of the political system and Nazarbayev personally, declaring that the president's tenure was illegitimate (Kazhegeldin, 1998b). At the same time, Kazhegeldin established a political party, The Republican Peoples Party of Kazakhstan (RPNK), to use as a public platform to drive forward his political ambitions (D'yachenko et al., 2000, 101). In creating the RNPK, and in declaring his intention to stand in the presidential election, Kazhegeldin had clearly moved from being loyal to the regime and only using internal voice to exiting the regime and evoking voice publicly. The former Prime Minister was the first politician in post-Soviet Kazakhstan to seriously announce their ambitions vis-à-vis Nazarbayev (Muminov, 2015).[10]

DVK was created in November 2001 by a public statement to the press after its participants, a set of young leading political elites and businessmen (see Table 5.1), had already sought to place internal pressure on Nazarbayev to rein in the behaviour of his son-in-law, Rakhat Aliyev. Many of those involved in the creation of DVK were known as 'The Young Turks'. They were Western-educated, young, and ambitious elites who had been promoted to senior positions within government by Nazarbayev in the mid-to-late 1990s. Their disaffection was driven by their perception that Nazarbayev did 'not live up to his promises on political reform'[11] and his failure to 'provide equal competition for all

---

[10] While Serikbolsyn Abdil'din, and to an extent Olzhas Suleimenov, could be considered the earliest political opponents of Nazarbayev (see previous chapter), as they were respective leaders of The Communist Party of Kazakhstan and the Party of Peoples Congress of Kazakhstan, neither represented a serious challenge to his Presidency during the 1990s.

[11] Author's interview Vladimir Kozlov.

representatives'.[12] The political and economic system which had developed in Kazakhstan did not match the spirit of economic liberalism many of them were wedded to and had signed up for in joining the government in the 1990s. Instead, competition for control of businesses and political positions had become corrupt and prone to cronyism with preference given to Nazarbayev's family.[13] The unity underpinning the DVK movement did not last long, and the group splintered into two political parties DVK (led by Zhakiyanov and Ablyazov) and *AK Zhol* (Bright Path) (led by Abilov and Baimenov). As discussed below, the fracturing of the movement was a consequence of the different choices available to these oligarchic opposition elites, which in turn was conditioned by a fear of sanctions.

There are two other notable cases where political elites have exited the regime while also exhibiting voice. In both cases, there is no evidence of internal regime voice prior to the exit, but it cannot be ruled out. The first was former Prosecutor General and ex-Speaker of the *Mazhilis*, Zharmakhan Tuyakbai, who in 2004 just after the parliamentary elections in which he topped the parliamentary list for the president's party, *Otan*, resigned his position as speaker and condemned the conduct of the elections. Critics of Tuyakbai have noted that his disaffection with the system, and thus his exit plus public voice, was down to personal ambition and a perceived belief that he was about to lose his position as Speaker of the *Mazhilis* (Kazinform, 2004).[14]

The second case concerns the *enfant terrible* of Kazakhstani politics, Rakhat Aliyev. Aliyev transformed from in-favour son-in-law to Nazarbayev's enemy number one because of his alleged involvement in the kidnapping of two directors of one of Kazakhstan's leading banks, Nurbank. Aliyev allegedly attempted to force the directors into handing control of the bank over to him. That Aliyev's kidnapping scandal came to light at all in what is a state-dominated media, indicated that all was not well within the regime and Nazarbayev family relations. The president ordered the Prosecutor General and the Minster of Internal Affairs to investigate the alleged kidnapping and in response Aliyev went into

[12] The equal competition of representatives which is being referred to concerns the direct elections of regional *Akims* rather than them being appointed by the president. Author's interview with Galymzhan Zhakiyanov.

[13] Author's interview with Galymzhan Zhakiyanov.

[14] Author's interview with political analyst, 18 May 2007, Almaty, Kazakhstan.

Table 5.1 Signatures to the creation of DVK, 18 November 2001

Name	Position
G. Zhakiyanov	Akim of Pavlodar Oblast
U. Zhandosov	Deputy Prime Minister
N. Subkhanberdin	Chairman of Kazkommertsbank
M. Ablyazov	Ex-Energy Minister and Head of Astana-Holdings
A. Ashimov	Director and Actor
T. Tokhtasynov	Mazhilis Deputy
B. Abilov	Mazhilis Deputy and member of the Political Council of Otan
S. Konakbaev	Mazhilis Deputy
Z. Ertlesova	Deputy Defence Minister
A. Baimenov	Minister of Labour and Social Protection
B. Imashev	Chairman of the Anti-Monopoly Agency
K. Kelimbetov	Deputy Finance Minister
T. Alzhanov	Chairman of the Investment FM
S. Esimkhanov	Senate Deputy
G. Amrin	Deputy Secretary of the Security Council
Z. Battalova	Senate Deputy
A. Mashani	Senate Deputy
N. Smagulov	President of Kazprodkorporatsii
I. Meltser	Editor in chief of Vremya
E. Tatishev	Chairman of Turan Alem

hiding in Vienna (where he was already based). The Kazakhstani government's attempts to extradite Aliyev back to Kazakhstan failed, while the president's daughter, Dariga Nazarbayeva, was forced to divorce her now out of favour husband. Aliyev claimed that the reason his father-in-law moved against him was that he confirmed to the president in a private conversation he would run for the presidency in 2012. Aliyev was not, and could not be considered political opposition. DVK emerged precisely into opposition 'because of their reluctance to submit to a rigid system which Aliyev was involved in constructing' (Satpayev, 2015). Once his alleged involvement in the kidnapping scandal became public, Aliyev exited the regime (through being dismissed from his position at the time as Ambassador to the OSCE in Vienna) and the country at the same time equalling scenario where Aliyev exited nodal points 1 and 3 of the exit, voice and loyalty matrix simultaneously while also using voice. Aliyev only became an open critic of the Nazarbayev regime once charges were brought against him and the government sought his extradition back to Kazakhstan (Lillis, 2007). Considering this, Aliyev's agency was limited. The severest form of sanctions had already been applied (a politically motivated judicial process) and thus loyalty to his father-in-law represented no tangential benefits, while appealing to a democratic discourse and a Western audience, despite his best efforts to undermine democratic practice in the country until that point, represented the optimum strategy for his political and personal survival.

The above examples of exit and voice (both private and public voice internal and external to the regime) of political elites in Kazakhstan demonstrate there are two broad reasons for why elites may choose to use public voice, and therefore take the nodal point of exit from the regime. The first relates to issues of political and personal enmity arising from the oligarchic and personalist relations in the country. Opposition elites feel the system of authority as its exists provides them with inadequate opportunities to realise either their political or economic ambitions.[15] The second are broader contextual factors often linked to contingency such as: economic crisis[16] (emergence of Kazhegeldin) and the consequence of earlier reforms offering a new tranche of liberal and reform-minded elites (DVK and the 'Young Turks'). Nevertheless, once opposition elites have taken the first step of exiting from the regime and evoking public voice, the extent to which they continue to use that voice, and whether they revert to a form of loyalty to the regime, is conditioned by actual and potential sanctions, and most significantly institutional adaptation.

Sanctions and Institutional Adaptation and Nodal Point 3 Exit the Political System/Country

In his decision to exit the regime and evoke a public denunciation of the political system, Akezhan Kazhegeldin had no prior knowledge of the type of sanctions that the regime would eventually apply to his perceived disloyalty. The sanctions applied to Kazhegeldin were individual and organisational alongside institutional adaptation which sought to alter the architecture of the political space. The effect of the sanctioning process was that Kazhegeldin proceeded to the third nodal point and exited the country to live in exile in Europe.

---

[15] Author's interview Amirzhan Kosanov.

[16] Kazhegeldin's emergence into opposition coincided with the 1998 financial crisis in Kazakhstan, itself a product of the Russian financial crisis.

The initial individual sanction instigated against Kazhegeldin was that he was barred from running in the 1999 presidential election on the grounds of a minor 'administrative offence' for participating in an unsanctioned demonstration (Fuller, 1999). This was coupled with an alleged campaign of *Chernyi piar* (black PR),[17] through major media channels, led from within the Komitet Natsional'noi Bezaopasnosti (Security Services [KNB]), which set out to discredit Kazhegeldin, as well as a campaign to outlaw and destroy copies of his book in the country (Akkuly, 2010). The final, and fatal, personal sanction was the filing of three criminal cases against the ex-Prime Minister by the Tax Police (led by Rakhat Aliyev) on grounds of corruption, tax evasion, money laundering and the illegal purchase of property in Belgium (Shurga, 1999). Kazhegeldin and his supporters have always maintained the charges were politically motivated (Press Service of RNPK, 2001). Individual sanctions were also applied to close associates of Kazhegeldin who found themselves under the threat of violence, intimidation, and detention such as Amirzhan Kosanov, former Deputy Minister for Youth, Tourism and Sport, and Kazhegeldin's press secretary while Prime Minister (Akkuly, 2010).[18]

Organisational sanctions were also applied to RNPK in relation to their participation in the 1999 parliamentary elections. The party encountered difficulties in campaigning and gaining access to the media.[19] Most importantly in organisational terms, in response to the emergence of RPNK as a political platform to support the political ambitions of Kazhegeldin, Nazarbayev and the presidential administration created a new pro-presidential party, *Otan* (Fatherland), from a series of smaller parties to support the political programme of the president (D'yachenko et al., 2000, 79; Isaacs, 2011, 72–73). *Otan* not only went on to dominate the 1999 election, but also in its later formulation as *Nur Otan* (Light of Fatherland) it had complete control of legislative politics in the country, only strengthening the president's grip on the legislative agenda (Isaacs & Whitmore, 2014).

---

[17] *Chernyi piar* is a term which is particular to Russian, and broader Eurasian politics. It relates to the use of compromising information and incriminating evidence which is used through open media sources in a campaign to discredit particular individuals.

[18] Author's interview Amirzhan Kosanov.

[19] For examples of the difficulties the party faced in campaigning see the Commission on Security and Cooperation in Europe Report on the Parliamentary Elections in Kazakhstan October 10, 1999. Washington, DC: CSCE.

Kazhegeldin's foray into opposition politics also ignited at least two forms of institutional adaptation that were aimed either directly at him, RPNK or other potential opposition movements. The first was the introduction in 1998 of a Law on Enforcement Proceedings and Status of Court Bailiffs. Articles 79 and 80 of the law guaranteed the government's right to enforce court proceedings against citizens residing abroad. Close associates of the former Prime Minister argued that his provision within the law 'was designed specifically for Kazhegeldin'.[20] The second form of institutional adaptation pertained to changes to the electoral law which were introduced prior to the 1999 parliamentary election. While the headline-grabbing changes to the electoral law in 1999 included the introduction of a proportional element to the electoral system for the first time (10 seats within the legislature were awarded on a party-list basis), it was minor amendments to the law which represented a specific institutional adaptation relating to the exit and voice of Kazhegeldin and the RPNK. These minor amendments included the introduction of barring candidates from standing for election if they had committed an administrative offence (used against Kazhegeldin) and the introduction of a $1000 registration fee for parliamentary candidates (Fuller, 1999). Such high fees were a deterrent for opposition members standing in single mandate constituencies.

A similar set of personal and organisational sanctions, along with institutional adaptation, can be observed in relation to those oligarchic elites involved in the emergence of DVK. At the same time, however, the DVK case also illustrates how such sanctions push some opposition elites back towards more loyal behaviour. All the signatories to the original DVK letter who held government positions were dismissed after the expression of public voice outside of the regime. The two main leaders of DVK, Galymzhan Zhakiyanov and Mukhtar Ablyazov were arrested, convicted and sentenced on corruption charges to six and seven years in prison, respectively. Members of DVK also saw some of their economic assets stripped, such as Ablyazov and his stake in Bank Turan Alem (BTA) (Chebotarev, 2006). The heavy-handed nature of the personal sanctions upon Zhakiyanov and Ablyazov saw other members of DVK take a more emollient approach to the regime and Nazarbayev. Bolat Abilov, Oraz Zhandosov and Alikhan Baimenov set up a new political party, *AK Zhol*

---

[20] Author's interview Amirzhan Kosanov.

(Bright Path), which aimed to be more constructive and acquiescent with power and 'believed opposition elites should be polite to the president, constructive and to get an agreement with *vlast* (authorities)'.[21] This elite strategy is exit + voice + [potential] sanctions = exit with reduced voice. For Zhakiyanov imprisonment was an effective sanction on the part of the regime. He was released from prison on the grounds that he would refrain from being involved in politics. Zhakiyanov held his end of the bargain and on his release from prison kept out of politics and instead set up a Civil Society NGO. Ablyazov also made the same plea bargain, but seemingly found it difficult to keep away from politics as he was alleged to have funded the DVK 'Alga' political party (a successor party to DVK) and the opposition newspaper *Respublika* (Sindelar, 2013).[22] As noted below, this ended in serious difficulty for Ablyazov. In 2009, after the state took control of BTA, which he had re-joined as Chairman, Ablyazov found himself subject to legal proceedings for the misappropriation of $6 billion dollars of BTA funds (Gorst, 2013).

The major form of institutional adaptation which was introduced because of the emergence of DVK, and *AK Zhol* pertains to the 2002 Law on Political Parties. This law[23] put in place significant administrative barriers which parties were required to meet for registration with the Ministry of Justice, and therefore, allow them to compete in elections.[24] Some members of *AK Zhol* believed that revised law on political parties was a direct response to their emergence and 'was created against the party'.[25] All existing political parties had to re-register under the new law. However, while *AK Zhol* managed to navigate the tough new restrictions (as did DVK), Kazhegeldin's RPNK was denied registration based on 'invalid documentation' (Nomad, 2004). However, some restrictions inherent to the law such as any party failing to compete in two successive parliamentary elections would be de-registered automatically were used

---

[21] Author's interview with Assylbek Kozhakhmetov.

[22] Author's interview with local political analyst, 20 November 2006, Almaty, Kazakhstan.

[23] The original Law on Political Parties had been introduced in 1996.

[24] An example of these restrictions included parties to have at least 50,000 members, of which at least 700 must be in each of the 14 regions plus 2 city regions. This was a significant jump from the 3000 members required under the previous iteration of the law.

[25] Author's interview with an anonymous member of AK Zhol Party, 18 January 2007, Almaty, Kazakhstan.

against a successor party to *AK Zhol* (see below). The 2002 Law on Political Parties became an essential tool of the Nazarbayev regime to stymie efforts on the part of these oligarchic elites to re-establish institutional opposition in Kazakhstan.

Organisational sanctions against DVK and *AK Zhol* corresponded to the unfair and arbitrary treatment the parties received *vis-à-vis* their participation in the 2004 parliamentary elections. For example, Abilov was disbarred from standing on the basis of a conditional court sentence for slander, DVK and *AK Zhol* candidates for electoral commissions were discriminated against with most places going to pro-presidential parties, while the DVK, participating in a bloc with the Communist Party, faced 'a pattern of interference that hindered its ability to convey its message to the electorate…this pattern included detentions of DVK activists by police…and interference from local authorities in holding campaign events in several instances' (OSCE/ODHIR, 2004, 11). Candidates, officials, and members of both *AK Zhol* and DVK faced continued pressure of intimidation and violence from state enforcement agencies and sometimes unknown assailants.[26] The election of 2004 proved to be a turning point for many of the oppositional elites involved in the original DVK movement.

In the aftermath of the election the party was banned by the authorities for minor infringements to the Law on Political Parties (Procuror.kz, 2004). What was left of the DVK movement established the party *Alga* (Forward). Allegedly funded by Ablyazov, *Alga* never received registration and was eventually banned outright in 2012 after an Almaty court declared the organisation extremist, and after its leader Vladimir Kozlov had been sentenced to a seven-and-a-half-year prison term for seeking to overthrow the government as part of the riots and violence in Zhanaozen in 2011 (Lillis, 2012a, 2012b) (see following chapter).[27]

The continued pressure from sanctions in their varying forms led some opposition elites to alter their strategy in terms of exit, voice and loyalty. For example, after the 2004 parliamentary election *AK Zhol* split. Despite a well-funded campaign, and the belief that they had accrued large numbers of votes across the country, the party ended up with only

---

[26] Author's interview Amirzhan Kosanov.

[27] In December 2011 in Zhanaozen, a town in the Mangystau Region, striking oil workers clashed with police leading to violence and gunfire with 14 protestors shot dead.

one member of parliament. For senior members of the party 'the elections had been falsified and the results taken away from the party'.[28] The party split over how best to respond to rigging of the electoral system in favour of the president and his party (Taukina, 2005). Alikhan Baimenov opted for loyalty and took up the only seat *AK Zhol* had been awarded in the *Mazhilis*. Abilov, Zhandosov, alongside former ministers Altynbek Sarsenbayev and Tulegen Zhukeev created *Nagiz AK Zhol* (Real Bright Path). This split was solidified in the 2005 presidential elections where Baimenov and *AK Zhol* failed to support the united opposition candidate, Zharmakhan Tuyakbai. Baimenov's move back to loyalty from a position of exit + voice ensured his political survival and that of *AK Zhol*. Baimenov eventually came full circle and took up a position in government in 2011 as Chairman of the Civil Service Agency, a position he had held previously in the late 1990s. The new leader of *AK Zhol* in 2011 was Azat Peruashev. He was formerly head of the pro-presidential Civic Party of Kazakhstan, until it was merged into *Nur Otan* in 2006, of which he was also a member. *AK Zhol* had gone from opposition party to being fully co-opted by the regime. In 2012, 2016 and 2021 it won 8, 7 and 12 seats, respectively, in the legislative elections to the *Mazhilis*, but the party is no longer understood as an opposition party. The leadership of *Nagiz AK Zhol* endured years of intermittent arrests, a complete failure to breakthrough electorally, because of a rigged electoral system, and even murder.[29] In February 2006 Altynbek Sarsenbayev was found murdered on a road outside of Almaty. While there is no evidence the authorities in Kazakhstan were specifically responsible for ordering his killing, KNB security servicemen were found guilty of the murder, it does highlight the highest potential cost for using voice in opposition politics in Kazakhstan. Likewise, Zamanbek Nurkadilov was also found dead a year after he had declared his opposition to Nazarbayev in 2004 and soon after he claimed he was going to release information detailing corruption at the heart of the Nazarbayev regime. His death was ruled as a suicide, but given he

---

[28] Author's interview with Tulegen Zhukeev former co-chairman of *Nagiz AK Zhol*, 21 February 2007, Almaty, Kazakhstan.

[29] In an interview with Bolat Abilov in 2011 he detailed the ways in which the electoral system and inherent practices inherent to it have interfered with his party's ability to campaign and compete fairly in elections. Author's interview with Bolat Abilov, former leader of Nagiz AK Zhol and Azat parties, 12 July 2011, Almaty, Kazakhstan.

had two gunshot wounds to the head it has fuelled speculation that he was murdered (Kusainov, 2005).

After the 2004 election Abilov, Zhandosov and Zhukeev cooperated with Zharmakhan Tuyakbai who was put forward as the united opposition's candidate for the 2005 presidential election, which he lost badly (Nazarbayev obtained 91% of the vote). Tuyakbai's party *Obshchnatsional'noi sotsial-demokraticheskoi partii* (All-National Social Democratic Party [OSDP]) joined forces with *Nagiz AK Zhol*, now named *Azat* (Freedom) for the 2007 parliamentary elections. The parties had tried to compete in an electoral bloc. However, the introduction of another institutional sanction by way of changes to the electoral legislation which forbade parties from combining in electoral blocs put a stop to any attempt of the parties to unite for the election without formally having to merge as single political party, which they subsequently had to do renaming themselves as Azat-OSDP. The merged party had no electoral success winning just 4.5 per cent in the 2007 election and no seats (Nur Otan won all the seats), 1.68 per cent in the 2012 election and 1.18 per cent in the 2016 election (the party boycotted the 2021 election).

Realising the failure of the voice to alter the political situation in the country, and under pressure from the numerous sanctions placed upon them individually and organisationally and through institutional adaptation, opposition elites gradually disappeared from the political scene moving from exit + voice to exit − voice. Oraz Zhandosov left politics after the election in 2007 and returned to being an economist, setting up his own analytical foundation, RAKURS and his own Joint Stock Company, the DAMU Entrepreneurship Development Fund. After being excluded again on administrative grounds from running in the 2012 parliamentary election as part of Azat-OSDP, Abilov announced in September 2013 that he was ceasing all political activities and going into television and film work. While he gave no specific reason for his departure from politics, Abilov's move to a strategy of exit without voice was believed to be conditioned by the years of sanctions placed upon him and that he was tired of spending his energy on realising political ambitions which now seemed fruitless (Muminov, 2013).[30] Abilov's exit from the political scene left Zharmakhan Tuyakbai the leader of the lone opposition movement. However, ever since Tuyakbai held a meeting with

---

[30] Author's interview Amirzhan Kosanov, former member of the Republican Peoples Party of Kazakhstan & OSDP, 25 February 2016, Almaty, Kazakhstan.

Nazarbayev in 2006, the impression was created that the former speaker of the Parliament was a loyal servant of the president, and that he was not serious about political opposition and was seeking to cut a deal with *vlast* (Baitov, 2006).[31] Whether this is true or not, as noted above, OSDP continued to fare poorly in electoral terms. Electoral performance has much to do with the broader political context in which the state and media outlets are set up to support the president's party *Nur Otan*, at the expense of all other political parties (Isaacs, 2011, 80–85).[32] However, in the view of one member of the OSDP-Azat Political Council, the regime ignores the party. It pays no attention to the statements and policies it issues and 'acts like it does not exist'.[33] Silence on the part of the regime with regard to the activities of OSDP acts as a form of sanction as it gives it no additional public attention starving it of publicity and legitimation as a relevant political force in society. The silence from the regime drove the party and Tuyakbai to the margins of political life in the country. Tuyakbai stood down as Chairman in 2019 ahead of the new presidential elections in the wake of Nazarbayev's resignation. He was replaced in April 2019 by Yermurat Bapi, a newspaper editor and former member of Kazhegeldin's RPNK, who was then replaced only four months later by Askat Rakhymzhanov in what was described as an illegal take-over of the party by Bergey Ryskaliev, the former *Akim* of the Atyrau region (Darimbet, 2019). Under Rakhymzhanov's leadership the party voted to boycott the 2021 parliamentary election (Radio Azattyk, 2020).

The above analysis demonstrates that a number of opposition elites—among them Zhakiyanov, Baimenov, Zhandosov and Abilov all chose, after different periods of time, and after numerous forms of sanctions, to switch from exiting the regime with voice, to either returning to the regime with no voice, in other words loyalty (as in the case of Baimenov), or remaining within the country but no longer expressing concerns and complaints regarding the political system and relinquishing all political ambitions. It exemplifies the way in which sanctions and institutional adaptation conditioned and shaped the strategic choices of oligarchic opposition in Kazakhstan. In the cases of Akezhan Kazhegeldin, Rakhat

---

[31] Author's interview with local political analyst, 26 February 2016, Almaty, Kazakhstan.

[32] Author's interview with Bolat Abilov; author's interview with Amirbek Togissov, Member of OSDP Political Council, 4 April 2012, Almaty, Kazakhstan.

[33] Author's interview with Member of OSDP Political Council, 23 February 2016, Almaty, Kazakhstan.

Aliyev and Mukhtar Ablyazov, the criminal proceedings brought against them forced their hand in terms of exiting Kazakhstan (in Aliyev's case he was already out of the country as Kazakhstan's ambassador to the OSCE in Vienna). In each case the Kazakhstani government sought extradition and except for Ablyazov (his extradition process is still on-going) all efforts failed. Kazhegeldin and Aliyev were tried and convicted in absentia. All three have continued to criticise the authoritarian regime of Nazarbayev while in exile, Aliyev did so with great fanfare, publishing in 2009 *The God Father-in-law*, a lengthy book providing a detailed account of his allegations regarding the corrupt nature of the Nazarbayev regime. After a four-year investigation into the charges of kidnapping, the Viennese authorities arrested Aliyev in 2014 when he handed himself in to cooperate with the investigation. He was found dead in his prison cell in February 2015, reportedly having committed suicide from hanging, although Aliyev's lawyer claims the circumstances of his death were suspicious (Paterson, 2015). Kazhegeldin has managed to live safely in London since he left Kazakhstan in 1999, and there are often reports he is seeking to begin a dialogue with authorities to negotiate his return to the country (Muminov, 2015) and Kazhegeldin continues to comment frequently on Kazakhstani politics (Turgaev, 2022). Perhaps his ability to survive has been tempered by the less sharp criticisms he has drawn of Nazarbayev than that of Ablyazov and Aliyev.

Conclusion: Feedback Signals and Authoritarian Durability and Instability

The story of oligarchic opposition from 1998 onwards in Kazakhstan is not just a story of a moribund political opposition (Muminov, 2013), it is also the story of the failure to re-establish institutional opposition in Kazakhstan after Nazarbayev's consolidation of power in 1995 (see previous chapter). In more abstract terms the relations between oligarchic opposition and the regime in Kazakhstan also informs our understanding of the influence of exit and voice—as forms of opposition agency—on the stability of authoritarian regimes, particularly in cases where the regime treats the threat from the opposition in an ambiguous manner.

In the case of Kazakhstan, elite exit from the regime while increasing short-term political instability provides an important feedback signal for regime stability in the medium to longer term. The regime adjusts to the signal by recalibrating resources, introducing sanctions against potential threats and changing the law to try and stop further political opposition. For example, the 2002 Law on Political Parties created a very restrictive environment which made it practically impossible for new opposition parties to register. The only new opposition party that emerged and received registration after the introduction of the law was Tuyakbai's OSDP (which is one of the reasons some people in the country were suspicious of Tuyakbai's relations with the presidential administration). The signal of discontent from the fragmenting elites in the period 1998–2007 provided the regime with a stimulus to react and contain the opposition threat to its power. Therefore, the decision of opposition elites to exit and use public voice—rather than destabilising the regime—seemingly strengthened it.

The regime also uses the feedback signal from opposition agency of exit and voice to also adopt the language and policy of reform to weaken the claims of opposition movements and parties, and thus to steal the mantle of political transformation. This was most notable after the emergence of DVK and *AK Zhol*. These two parties changed the discourse within Kazakhstani politics to one which was about political reform. In response to these demands, the presidential administration set up a series of commissions from 2001 to 2006 to explore the issue of reforming the political system (Isaacs, 2008). This eventually led to constitutional changes in 2007 which in the view of the presidential administration represented a shift to a presidential-parliamentary system, thus devolving power from Nazarbayev's hands to the formal institutions of the state, and as such taking the sting out of the demands of the opposition. The reforms were, however, for the most part cosmetic, and amounted to the minimal amount of change which could be undertaken so as not to unsettle or create further threats to the regime. The regime, therefore, took ownership of the discourse of democracy and political reform, using the language of the opposition, but adopting and shaping it to its own ends. The idea of 'Kazakhstan's path to democracy' developed as a fundamental part of the regime's discourse of its own legitimation (Balgimbayev, 2013). This has been possible because of the feedback signal generated by the different choices of exit and voice adopted by the political opposition in Kazakhstan.

The paradox, however, is that while the regime has used opposition agency as a feedback signal to correct its course which aided regime durability by seeing off threats to its position, it did so by closing off future feedback signals. This paradox can be understood through the way in which the regime treated the oligarchic opposition in an ambiguous way. The regime understood oligarchic opposition as credible enough to act against the perceived threat from Kazhegeldin and DVK through means of personal and organisational sanctions, and institutional adaptation. Yet, at the same time the opposition was not seen as credible enough to co-opt back into the regime. By failing to see opposition threats as wholly credible, the regime over-relied on coercive practices of sanctions and institutional adaptation. While such acts on part of the regime insulated it from the initial opposition threat, it fails to have the desired effect of regime stability. By failing to institutionalise the oligarchic opposition through co-optation the regime created wider discontent, but this time more grassroots, spontaneous and activist based. From 2011 onward the regime faced a series of 'shocks' that challenged its stability. These were spontaneous and largely grassroots protest movements that were in essence difficult for the regime to see coming because of the closure of the feedback loop provided by opposition agency of exit and voice. These forms of non-oligarchic voice as a form of opposition agency are the subject of the next chapter.

References

Akkuly, S. (2010, November 24). U Rakhat Alieva trebyut kompensatsiyu za repressii i stradaniya v tyur'me. *Radio Azattyk*. Accessed online 7 Jan 2022. https://rus.azattyq.org/a/afanasenko_officer_Kazakhstan_civill_action_rakhat_alyev_/2228151.html

Alzhanov, M. (2004, December 3). Politicheskaya 'bomba; Zamanbeka Nurkadilova. *Respublika*. Accessed 27 June 2008. http://www.iwww.kub.info/article.php?sid=5522

Baitov, R. (2006, September 22). Kak Zh Tuyakbai s prezidentom vstrechalsya. *Nomad*. Accessed 31 Mar 2016. http://www.nomad.su/?a=3-200609 220227

Balgimbayev, B. (2013, August 31). Kazakhstanskaya model' demokratii: stanovlenie i spetsifika. *Mezhdunarodnaya Akademiia Informatizatsii*. Accessed 7 June 2014. http://academy.kz/ru/normativnye-akty/entry/kazakhstanskaya-model-demokratii-stanovlenie-i-spetsifika

Chebotarev, A. (2006, November 7). Politicheskii krizis oseni 2011 goda i ego posledstviya 5 let spustya. *Kub*. Accessed 14 Dec 2006. http://www.kub.info/article.php?sid=15070

Darimbet, N. (2019, October 8). Ermurat Bali: novyi khozyin OSDP – beglyi oligarkh, kz.media. Accessed 26 Jan 2022. https://kz.media/archives/2499

D'yachenko, S., Karmazina, L., and Seidumanov, S. (2000). *Politicheskie partii Kazakhstana god 2000 spravochnik*. Information-Analttical Centre of the Parliament of Kazakhstan.

Eurasian Transition Group. (2009). *The Aliev Dossier*. ETG.

Fuller, L. (1999, September 18). Kazakhstan's Kazhegeldin conspicuous by his absence. *Asia Times*. Accessed 29 Mar 2016. http://www.atimes.com/c-asia/AI18Ag02.html

Gorst, I. (2013, July 5). Mukhtar Ablyazov at centre of fight over Kazakhstan's BTA Bank. *Financial Times*. Accessed 31 Mar 2016. http://www.ft.com/cms/s/0/23571482-e584-11e2-ad1a-00144feabdc0.html#axzz3wCYbKtZ7

Isaacs, R. (2008). Managing dissent, limiting risk and consolidating power: The processes and results of constitutional reform in Kazakhstan. *Central Asia and the Caucasus, 44*(1), 16–25.

Isaacs, R. (2011). *Party system formation in Kazakhstan: Between formal and informal politics*. Routledge.

Isaacs, R., & Whitmore, S. (2014). The limited agency and life-cycles of personalized dominant parties in the post-Soviet space: The cases of United Russia and Nur Otan. *Democratization, 21*(4), 699–721.

Junisbai, B. (2010). (2010) A tale of two Kazakhstans: Sources of political cleavage and conflict in the post-Soviet period. *Europe-Asia Studies, 62*(2), 235–269.

Kazhegeldin, A. (1998a). *Kazakhstan: pravo vybora*. Karzhy Karzhat.

Kazhegeldin, A. (1998b). *Akezhan Kazhegeldin announces candidacy for the presidency of Kazakhstan*. Accessed 29 Mar 2016. http://www.prnewswire.com/news-releases/akezhan-kazhegeldin-announces-candidacy-for-the-presidency-of-kazakhstan-76947707.html

Kazinform. (2004, October 19). Zharmakhan Tuyakbai zayavil o vykhode is partii Otan. *Nomad*. Accessed 25 Mar 2016. http://www.nomad.su/?a=3-200410190019

Kusainov, A. (2005, November 13). Mysterious murder mars presidential election campaign. *Eurasianet*. Accessed 2 Apr 2016. http://www.eurasianet.org/departments/insight/articles/eav111405.shtml

Lillis, J. (2007, June 12). The domestic implications of Rakhat Aliev's precipitous fall. *Eurasianet*. Accessed 13 June 2007. http://www.eurasianet.org/departments/insight/articles/eav061307f.shtml

Lillis, J. (2012a, October 10). Kazakhstan: Political trial fails to provoke Pussy Riot-Style outcry. *Eurasianet*. Accessed 31 Mar 2016. http://www.eurasianet.org/node/66330

Lillis, J. (2012b, December 21). Kazakhstan: Court shuts key opposition party. *Eurasianet*. Accessed 31 Mar 2016. http://www.eurasianet.org/node/66032

Muminov, A. (2013). Oppozitsiya v Kazakhstane. Klient, ckoree, mertv, Kursiv, 20 September. Accessed 4 December 2013. http://www.kursiv.kz/news/obs hestvo/Oppozitciya-v-Kazahstane-Klientskoree-mertv/

Muminov, A. (2015, April 24). Vechnoe vozvrashchenie – Akezhana Kazhegeldina prizovut v preddverii cereznykh reform? *Kursiv*. Accessed 16 May 2015. http://www.kursiv.kz/news/vlast/vechnoe_vozvrashchenie_akez hana_kazhegeldina_prizovut_v_preddverii_sereznykh_reform_916/

Nomad. (2004, May 12). V Kazakhstane likvidrovany chetyre parti. *nomad*. Accessed 12 Oct 2008. http://www.nomad.su/?a=3-200405120021

OSCE/ODHIR. (2004). *Republic of Kazakhstan parliamentary elections 19 September and 3 October 2004: OSCE/ODIHR election observation mission report*. OSCE/ODIHR.

Paterson. (2015, March 15). Rakhat Aliyev: Claims of murder over death of rival to Kazakhstan's president in Austrian prison. *The Independent*. Accessed 31 Mar 2016. http://www.independent.co.uk/news/world/asia/rakhat-ali yev-claims-of-murder-over-death-of-rival-to-kazakhstans-president-in-an-aus trian-prison-10108693.html

Press Service of RNPK. (2001, September 7). Zaochnyi sud nad Kazhegeldinym kak rezul'tat politiki bezzakoniia i proizvola. *Press Service of RNPK*. Accessed 26 June 2008. http://kazhegeldin.addr.com/articles/About_07_09_01_3.htm

Procuror.kz. (2004, December 13). Zayavlenie o likvidatsii yridicheskogo litsa. *Procuror.kz*. Accessed 3 May 2007. http://www.procuror.kz/?iid=5&type=news&lang=ru&nid=61

Radio Azattyk. (2020, November 27). OSDP pb'yavila boikot vyboram Ablyazov schitate, chto partyiya vypolnyaet 'prikaz'. *Radio Azattyk*. Accessed 26 Jan. https://rus.azattyq.org/a/kazakhstan-party-to-boycott-january-parlia mentary-elections/30971975.html

Satpayev, D. (2015, February 24). Rakhat Aliev ne predstavlyal ugrozy vlastyam Kazakhstana. *Kursiv*. Accessed 27 Feb 2015. http://www.kursiv.kz/news/ vlast/rakhat_aliev_ne_predstavlyal_ugrozy_vlastyam_kazakhstana_d_satpaev_ 166/

Shurga, S. (1999, September 25). Delo Kazhegel'dina prodolzhaetsya. *Nezavisi maya Gazeta*. Accessed online 7 Jan 2022. https://www.ng.ru/cis/1999-09-25/kazhegeldin.html

Sindelar, D. (2013, March 31). How far will Nazarbaev go to take down Mukhtar Ablyazov? *RFE/RL*. Accessed 2 Apr 2013. http://www.rferl.org/ content/kazakhstan-nazarbaev-ablyazov/25010488.html

Taukina R. (2005, April 29). Raskol v partii AK Zhol: Konflikt liderov ili idei? *Club Polyton*. Accessed 6 Oct 2006. http://www.club.kz/index.php?lang= en&mod=analitics&submod=self&article=310

Turgaev, S. (2022, January 6). Ya porazhayus' terpeniyu etogo naroda. Byvshii prem'er Kazakhstana – o prichinakh massovykh protestov v strane. *Nastoyashchee Vremya*. Accessed 11 Jan 2022. https://www.currenttime.tv/a/byvshiy-premyer-kazakhstana/31642149.html

CHAPTER 6

Non-oligarchic Public Voice in Kazakhstan from Below, 2011–2022

INTRODUCTION

The preceding two chapters have been largely concerned with forms of institutional opposition as they have appeared in Kazakhstan. The 1990s saw the foreclosing of the space for institutional opposition in the face of an emergent personalist authoritarian regime. The 2000s, on the other hand, saw attempts to re-establish an institutional opposition by oligarchic opposition groups. This oligarchic form of opposition tended to centre around specific individuals (e.g., Kazhegeldin, Ablyazov, etc.) who established party organisations as platforms to drive forward their political ambitions. With the decline of oligarchic opposition after the use of their agency through exit and voice, we are left to observe the fragments of opposition in Kazakhstan through the lens of non-institutional forms of opposition. Thus, this chapter seeks to capture examples of how in the absence of institutional opposition what instead appears is grassroots opposition voice which is channelled through trade unions, civic groups and individual activists. The form of opposition agency often appears spontaneously not least because in treating oligarchic institutional opposition in an ambiguous way, the Kazakhstani regime closed off the feedback loop which opposition agency provided through exit and voice. Consequently, Kazakhstani authorities were unable to grasp the preferences and interests of sections of the population resulting in a series of 'shocks' to

© The Author(s), under exclusive license to Springer Nature
Switzerland AG 2022
R. Isaacs, *Political Opposition in Authoritarianism*,
The Theories, Concepts and Practices of Democracy,
https://doi.org/10.1007/978-3-031-06536-1_6

the regime, the latest being the events of *qandy qantar* in 2022 which has been the most critical in terms of regime stability.

This chapter details these spontaneous 'shocks' demonstrating how non-oligarchic public voice destabilised the regime in Kazakhstan forcing it to recalibrate its position. The chapter analyses four instances of non-institutional grassroots opposition. The first in 2011 concerns a six-month strike by oil workers which eventually led to a bloody and fatal clash with the authorities on Independence Day in December of that year. The second was a series of large-scale protests in 2016 across Kazakhstan regarding proposals the government had put forward concerning land reform. As the chapter will detail, the land protests saw a climbdown from the government over the policy, illustrating the ways in which in authoritarian contexts opposition agency and voice can produce policy shifts and shape regime trajectories. The third example relates to a spate of protests which emerged after Nazarbayev announced his resignation in March 2019, handing power to his chosen successor, Kassym-Zhomart Tokayev. The so-called 'transition' incited a well-spring of grassroots, youth-led, political activism and protest demanding fair elections and a shift to a parliamentary system. The response from the Tokayev regime was to ostensibly introduce a modicum of political reform and to promote the idea of Kazakhstan being a 'listening state'. The failure of this as a strategy in addressing the concerns of citizens was evident in the fourth example of grassroots opposition which was the January protests of 2022 where a protest over a hike in energy prices led to widespread protests across the country taking on wider grievances concerning both the material conditions of citizens and issues pertaining to genuine political and democratic reform. The protests, however, took a dark turn when they were seemingly infiltrated by a violent criminal element and became entangled within intra-elite disputes.

The chapter addresses each of these cases in turn. Before that however it is worth addressing the nature of non-institutional opposition in Kazakhstan.

Non-institutional Opposition Agency in Kazakhstan: Non-oligarchic Voice

While this chapter will draw attention to four cases of grassroots-based opposition in Kazakhstan which emerged in a context where oligarchic institutional opposition had been foreclosed, this is not to say that these are the only four examples, nor that no forms of non-institutional opposition existed prior to the marginalisation of oligarchic opposition. As noted in Chapter 3, both in pre- and post-independent Kazakhstan there was a flourishing of civic-based, non-institutional forms of opposition (Ponomarev, 1991). However, the civil society context in which such groups emerged, evolved and operated within is one where the state undertook an activist role and played both a direct and indirect role in associational life, the sum of which ensured that groups genuinely critical of the regime were highly circumscribed (Ziegler, 2010, 799). The Kazakh authorities have taken up a considerable role in both setting up state-sponsored NGOs and in offering funds, publicity and recognition for those groups engaging in 'constructive cooperation' with the government (Makhmutova & Akhmetova, 2011, 20).

One of the defining features of the Nazarbayev regime's discourse about itself since independence has concerned its ability to provide stability for the country in contradistinction to the perceived instability in other countries in the Eurasian region, nominally Kyrgyzstan, Ukraine and Georgia (Koch, 2018; Kudaibergenova, 2019). However, this is a myth. While this chapter analyses four specific cases of spontaneous grassroots opposition protests in Kazakhstan, this is not to suggest that they have been the *only* instances of this type of opposition, nor that grassroots and spontaneous forms of non-institutional opposition *only* began with the marginalisation of oligarchic institutional opposition. Rather, throughout the 2000s and 2010s there were examples of non-oligarchic public voice against the regime which often appeared as forms of collective action. As Catherine Alexander (2018) has highlighted, protests over housing have been a persistent feature in the city of Almaty since the late 1980s. Most notably in 2006, residents in the Almaty micro-district Shanyrak resisted the city government's acquisition of land in the district which entailed the demolition of many houses and shacks (Alexander, 2018, 213). It led to violent clashes with the police and numerous human rights abuses including the denial of parole for some activists (Toguzbaev, 2018; Yessenova, 2010). Protests over housing continued into the next decade with a series of high-profile grassroots demonstrations taking place in 2016 against the spiralling costs of foreign currency mortgages (Toleukhanova, 2016a).

What the example of housing protests illustrate is that non-institutional opposition in Kazakhstan since 1991 is neither uniform nor homogenous. Grassroots opposition focuses on a range of issues that cut across class and other social cleavages in the country, but their claims can be broadly divided between the material and the ideational. The range of material claims includes issues pertaining to housing, access to land, ongoing labour disputes (Kumenov, 2021), access to social welfare provision (Lillis, 2019) and anti-debt resistance (Sanghera & Satybaldieva, 2021). Ideational claims, on the other hand, relate to broader themes of democracy, human rights, political reform, identity politics and social justice (Pron & Szwajnoch, 2019). This list is not exhaustive. The Oxus Society for Central Asian Affairs based in Washington, DC has been tracking protests in the region and found a range of issues as the basis on which protests emerge in Kazakhstan. In their report, the Oxus Society identified 520 cases of protests in Kazakhstan during a 20-month period between 2018 and 2020 which they identify as falling within ten categories, all of which could arguably be characterised as either representing material or ideational claims[1] (Jardine et al., 2021, 3–4).

The varied claims being made by grassroots opposition in Kazakhstan illustrate the heterogeneity of non-institutional opposition. There are many forms of public voice in Kazakhstan and the organised interests behind such voice are also varied. A potted overview of the types and forms of opposition over the last decade would include trade unions and organised labour strikes, especially in the oil and gas sector (Satpayev & Umbetaliyeva, 2015; Totaro & Sorbello, 2021), civic groups committed to political reform, such as *Oyan, Kazakhstan* (wake up, Kazakhstan) which emerged in 2019 in the aftermath of Nazarbayev's resignation and older democratic groups such as the DVK, who are supporters of the exiled oligarch Mukhtar Ablyazov (see previous chapter), and who are also banned and deemed a terrorist organisation by authorities (Mukhanov, 2018). But non-institutional opposition agency goes beyond any form of formal organisation such as trade unions and civic movements, as will be discussed below, the grassroots opposition which emerged in Kazakhstan in the last decade includes lone activists and spontaneous movements without any organising principle. For example, in 2019 a

---

[1] The ten categories are (with number of protests in parenthesis): human rights (214), justice (167), governance (140), livelihood (103), Covid 19 (74), property and land (70), China (57), Finance (19), environment and resource extraction (14) and other (13). Of all these categories, perhaps only Covid 19 protests stand out in terms of where they fit within the material vs. ideational binary, although arguably if Covid 19 protests concern issue of restricted liberty then they fall into the ideational.

group of mothers emerged as the unlikely face of dissent in their protests in response to a tragic fire which killed five children in the capital Astana, after the children had been left at home by the working parents. The tragedy spurred the mothers into making demands on the government to do more to support working mothers and families (Najibullah, 2019). Thus, this form of grassroots opposition is made up of different groups with varied interests and claims. While some groups possess organisational capacity, others appear without a clear organising principle and emerge in a spontaneous fashion because of deep-seated feelings of frustration and resentment with the quality and fairness of governance in Kazakhstan.

There are two further points to note about grassroots-based opposition before we proceed. Firstly, this broad conceptualisation of non-institutional form of opposition in Kazakhstan does not include criminal and violent groups. There have been a few instances in the last decade of violent terror like-attacks in the country. In 2011 a suicide bomber attacked the security service building in the city of Aktobe, in the northwest of the country. In the same province two police officers were also killed as part of an alleged terror attack (Lillis, 2011b). Similar violent attacks took place in Aktobe and Almaty in 2016 which left 22 people dead. The authorities claimed the attacks were undertaken by followers of a 'non-traditional religious movement' (Orazgaliyeva, 2016). Similarly, the violence which took place as part of the protests of January 2022 (see below) should equally not be equated with grassroots non-institutionalised opposition under discussion here. The dynamics of mobilisation and violence in January 2022 are equally complex, overlapping and opaque. Our concern here remains opposition which uses the strategy of voice (not violence) to signal to the regime deficiencies in government policy.

Secondly, the ability of grassroots opposition to mobilise is highly constrained. The laws pertaining to public assembly are very restrictive. Prior to 2019 and Tokayev becoming president, any individual or organisation seeking to hold a public rally or protest had to make a written request no later than 10 days in advance of the planned event to the local *Akim* (governor) who would decide whether to grant permission. Approval was typically given only to organisations and individuals perceived not to be critical of the regime. Opposition groups were usually denied permission to hold their rallies on spurious grounds.[2] Any unsanctioned protest was, and remains, against the law. As will be discussed below, the law was amended as a policy response to the 2019 election protests as Tokayev sought to mollify the concerns of protestors' demand for political reform. The revised law, introduced in 2020, now required groups to give 3–7 days' notice of a planned event to the local authorities, and then wait for approval (Rittmann, 2020). However, under the law, state authorities can restrict who protests and where. Only officially registered groups are allowed to submit notifications of rallies, and such events are only allowed to take place in officially designated spaces, and groups critical of the regime they are usually located far from the centre of the city (Pannier, 2020).

The following examples of the 2011, 2016, 2019 and 2022 protests will demonstrate how non-institutional grassroots opposition appeared in Kazakhstan as a series of 'shocks' to the regime. Ultimately each 'shock' emerged because the regime lacked the feedback signal which had previously existed with oligarchic opposition exit and voice. As the analysis illustrates below, the regime's efforts to respond by way of policy correction and sanctions have not succeeded in stymying discontent, again because of a failure to genuinely co-opt and bring in grassroots opposition, just like with the oligarchic opposition before. By treating opposition ambiguously in terms of their threat, the regime only serves to undermine its stability.

It is important to note that the analysis of the four cases below is not meant to be a definitive or even complete analysis of each event. A great deal has been published already on these events, especially in terms of more journalistic and policy-based accounts. Rather the purpose here is to simply demonstrate how opposition agency in Kazakhstan emerged in the fourth nodal point of the opposition-regime matrix. The four cases are used to illuminate the argument that with the decline of oligarchic institutional opposition agency, because of regime sanctions and institutional adaptation, the only place left for opposition agency to emerge was in this form of grassroots, often spontaneous, public voice.

---

[2] For example, rallies have been denied by the local city administration in Shymkent on the basis that the law states rallies cannot be held near a health care institution—and that proposed public assembly sites were near a pharmacy, which the authorities considered a health institution. This example is taken from the author's interview with Yevgenii Zhvotis, 31 January 2007, Almaty, Kazakhstan.

2011 Zhanaozen

The antecedents for the 2011 events in Zhanaozen, a town in Mangistau in Western Kazakhstan, began in 2010. Thousands of employees of Ozenmunaigaz (a subsidiary of KazMunaiGas, Kazakhstan's national oil company) took 19 days strike action over issues pertaining to changes to the wage system and the role of a manger in the imposition of those changes (Salmon, 2012, 73).[3] While the strike action of 2010 was settled, the economic issues underpinning them did not disappear. The Zhanaozen protests of 2011 centred on a labour dispute of thousands of oil workers at three companies: Ozenmunaigaz, Karazhanbasmunai (a joint Kazakh Chinese venture based close to the port city of Aktau) and Ersai Caspian Contractor (a joint Kazakh-Italian venture) (Satpayev & Umbetaliyeva, 2015, 126). The protests began at Karazhanbasmunai when workers initially went on hunger strike demanding parity of pay with workers at Ozenmunaigaz, who had won a settlement on wage increases because of their 19-day strike in 2010 (Salmon, 2011, 507). Activists called for a general strike across Mangistau. Kazakh workers at Ersai Caspian Contractor joined the protest and on 17th May 4500 workers walked out at Karazhanbasmunai. By the end of May workers from Ozenmunaigaz had also joined the strike and a local court declared the action illegal (Salmon, 2011, 507). The strike continued throughout the summer of 2011. While the demands from each workforce were varied, they largely centred on economic claims against the companies and the government. Leaders and activists of the unions supporting the striking workers were intimidated, persecuted and arrested by the authorities, while, Natalya Sokolova, a lawyer and trade union worker of Karazhanbasmunai was arrested, detained and put on trial for 'inciting social discord', receiving a six-year prison sentence (Glushkova, 2011; socialismkz.info, 2011). The local authorities sided with the companies who refused to cede to the workers' demands, declining to recognise informal labour unions.[4] Karazhanbasmunai and Ozenmunaigaz then sacked 2000 workers involved in the protest. While some workers had already returned

---

[3] This was not the first time there had been a strike at Ozenmunaigaz. A hunger strike had taken place in September 2009 regarding salary rises (Satpayev & Umbetaliyeva, 2015, 125).

[4] The companies insisted on only negotiating with the official Federation of Labour Unions of Kazakhstan which is seen as pro-government and thus not trusted by workers who instead established their own informal unions (Khamidov, 2011).

to work, those that remained established a 'tent city' in Zhanaozen's central square (Satpayev & Umbetaliyeva, 2015, 126). The protesters remained on the square throughout the autumn into December. During that period there were signs that the Kazakhstani government was considering intervening in the dispute because of the economic impact it was having on the oil sector (Lillis 2011a). Throughout, the demands of the workers differed from company to company, but broadly they were focused on economic not political claims including better pay and conditions and the right to organise trade unions independent from the pro-government Federation of Labour Unions of Kazakhstan (Pirani, 2021).

The protests turned violent on December 16, Kazakhstan's day of independence and the anniversary of the *Zheltoksan* events of 1986 (see Chapter 5). The violence began in Zhanaozen after the town authorities sought to clear the main square of protestors in preparation for independence day celebrations. While it is unclear how events unfolded, mass unrest ensued, and protestors tore up the stage being set up for the celebration. Rioting broke out between the protestors, local officials and the police, and a series of buildings, including the local government headquarters and offices of Ozenmunaigaz were set on fire (Lewis, 2016, 426). In response the police opened fire. The figure of how many died is disputed, the official government response was that 16 people died in the violence, but other reports suggest the number was much higher and evidence was reported of aggressive police behaviour in shooting unarmed citizens (Kostyuchenko, 2011). There were also reports that provocateurs dressed in KazMunaiGas uniforms were on the streets of Zhanaozen and provoked the riots deliberately (Yanovskaya & Kislov, 2012).[5] Nazarbayev then imposed a 20-day state of emergency in Zhanaozen that would last until January 5, 2012.

For a regime which had constructed a hegemonic discourse that Kazakhstan was a bastion of stability and prosperity, the event of December 2011 in Zhanaozen pierced the bubble of that narrative in two ways. Firstly, by illustrating that Kazakhstan was prone to civil unrest just like its neighbour Kyrgyzstan and secondly, that regime claims of economic

---

[5] Riots also broke out the next day at the railway station at Shetpe, a small village in Mangistau, where a group of people in support of the protestors in Zhanaozen set fire to a train—at least one person was reported dead, and a dozen were injured (see Al Jazeera, 2011).

prosperity were hollow in the face of the material claims made by the striking workers. Zhanaozen represented a different type of opposition to the regime than that it had faced from oligarchic exit and voice, but its response to the events continued to focus on sanctions and institutional adaptation.

Individual sanctions were placed upon those perceived to be the leaders of the protest. In June 2012, 34 oil workers were convicted on charges related to the mass unrest, with three, Rosa Tuletaeva, Maksat Dosmagambetov and Talgat Saktaganov sentenced to seven, six and four years, respectively, in prison, although it is believed that torture was used to divulge incriminating statements from the convicted (Human Rights Watch, 2012a; Lillis, 2012). But individual sanctions went beyond those actively involved in the protests. To establish an impression that local authorities too had to be sanctioned for their part in the violence and tragedy of Zhanaozen, Nazarbayev made a series of very public sackings of officials. The *Akim* of the Mangistau region, Krymbek Kusherbaev, was removed from his post,[6] but the president did not personally blame Kusherbaev for the events in Zhanaozen, instead he laid the blame for not resolving the labour dispute at the door of the Chairman of KazMunaiGas, Bolat Akchulakov, and Timur Kulibayev his son-in-law, head of the state sovereign wealth fund Samruk-Kazyna. Both were dismissed from their posts (Toguzbaev, 2011). Sanctions were also applied to political opponents of the regime who were not directly involved in the labour strikes. The regime sought to proportion blame for the mass unrest and violence on Mukhtar Ablyazov, somehow inciting unrest from outside of the country (Satpayev & Umbetaliyeva, 2015, 127). As noted in the previous chapter, the leader of the party Ablyazov was now believed to fund, *Alga* (forward), Vladimir Kozlov, was put on trial and sentenced to seven and a half years in prison for inciting social discord in relation to the events in Zhanaozen, along with two other activists (Human Rights Watch, 2012b).

---

[6] However, the Zhanaozen events did not end Krymbek Kusherbaev's career. Six months after his dismissal as *Akim* of Mangistau he was appointed as a special advisor to the president, then later deputy Prime Minister and *Akim* of the Kyzylorda region. Under Tokyaev's presidency, Kusherbaev was appointed to the position as head of the presidential administration and then state secretary, until he was fired during the bloody protests of January 2022.

Outside of placing sanctions on specific individuals, the regime sought to strengthen its institutional response to avoid such political instability in future. As Erica Marat has written, Nazarbayev 'ordered the strengthening and expansion of policing in rural areas, primarily by increasing intelligence to prevent demonstrations before they occur' (Marat, 2016, 540). Further institutional adaptation was undertaken to anticipate further labour unrest. In 2014 the government introduced a new trade union law which restricted the ability of worker to organise and form independent trade unions through a more rigorous registration process which forced local unions to affiliate with larger scale industrial unions, nominally the regime approved Federation of Labour Unions of Kazakhstan (Rittmann, 2021). In January 2017 the Confederation of Independent Trade Unions was also liquidated by a court in the South Kazakhstan Region over minor infringements to the registration procedures introduced as part of the 2014 trade union law (Trotsenko, 2017).[7]

Blame was also placed on one further group. According to Dosym Satpayev and Tolganay Umbetaliyeva, Kazakh ethnic repatriates, known as *oralman* (returnee), were blamed for the mass unrest in Zhanaozen (Satpayev & Umbetaliyeva, 2015, 127). As scholars have argued 'the events in Zhanaozen were framed through the prism of socioeconomic difficulties and linked to the challenges resulting from accepting many "Kazakhs" back in the country' (Beisembayeva et al., 2017, 49). In response to this developing narrative, the authorities sought to abandon the 'Nurly Kosh' (Bright Settlement) state programme for the resettlement of ethnic repatriates (Satpayev & Umbetaliyeva, 2015, 127).

The case of *oralman* demonstrates that the regime's response to grassroots non-oligarchic voice differed somewhat from its reaction to opposition agency via exit and voice in the late 1990s and 2000s simply by fact of its seeming ad-hoc and scattergun approach to addressing the events. The opposition was no longer a target in clear sight. The grassroots, spontaneous and collective nature of non-oligarchic opposition made addressing the threat harder to pin down. Thus, the regime sought to apply sanctions not just to some of those involved, but also to those not involved (Kozlov) and those within the regime itself (Kusherbaev, Akchulakov and Kulibayev), and even to whole groups (*oralman*) who

---

[7] Amendments were made to the law in 2020 which did ease the registration process for independent unions, removing the mandatory requirement that unions affiliate with a larger industrial body.

were perceived to have caused the disquiet in terms of their preferential treatment (in terms of the economic settlement package) that led to the unrest. Institutional adaptation through policing local populations and restricting labour rights was largely aimed as pre-emptive measures hoping to close off future potential unrest. The regime response ultimately possessed an extempore quality that sought to address probable threats to stability that were unknowable. The feedback signal which had been present during the preceding decade via oligarchic opposition exit and voice remained absent, leaving the regime in the dark about impending shocks. Further spontaneous unrest did appear again in 2016 in response to a regime policy towards land in Kazakhstan, a sacred issue for the Kazakh people.

2016 Land Protests

The land protests in Kazakhstan began when amendments to the land code were introduced in November 2015 which allowed for the long-term lease of agricultural land for up to 25 years to both Kazakhstani nationals and foreigners. This was an increase from 10 years which had been introduced in 2003 (Toleukhanova, 2016b). At the end of March 2016, Yerbolat Dosaev, Minister of the National Economy, announced that from July 2016 1.7 million hectares of agricultural land would be put up for auction. This announcement stoked discussion on social media sites with fears being raised that the amendments to the land code would allow foreigners to buy up land. Nominally the concern was with Chinese investors, and this led to an open public letter signed by representatives of the Kazakh intelligentsia 'on preventing the sale of land to foreigners' (Lakhanuly, 2015). Signs of broader public voice against the changes to the land code emerged with opposition to the amendments by a single activist in Astana. Galymbek Akulbekov held a one-man picket outside the *Mazhilis* (parliament) against 'the government's plan to sell land to foreigners'. While the picket lasted only five minutes before the police took Akulbekov away, it was a harbinger for what was to come in the next few days (Botaiuly, 2016). On April 24, 2016, in the city of Atyrau over a thousand people gathered to protest the changes to the land code which they perceived would mean the sale of Kazakh land to foreigners and the loss of sovereignty. The rally had not been sanctioned and the then local *Akim*, Nurlan Ozhaev, came out to explain to the crowd that the changes to the code did not threaten Kazakh sovereignty. After some hours the crowd dispersed peacefully (Toiken, 2016). In a space of a week further unsanctioned, seemingly uncoordinated, protests took place across major cities including Uralsk, Aktobe, Semey, Aktau, Zhanaozen, Kyzylorda and Pavlodar. These protests were not organised by political parties or opposition elites but by social activists who used social media to galvanise local populations against the proposed reform (Lillis, 2016a). The president sought to reassure the population when speaking to the Assembly of Peoples of Kazakhstan (APK) stating that 'the issue of selling state lands to foreign citizens is not worth, and is not, being discussed. All speculations on this topic are groundless' (Ferghana.ru, 2016).

Nazarbayev's comments did little to soothe the public discontent with the proposed changes. Even though the changes to the code did not mean that foreigners could buy land, in fact they could only lease it (only Kazakhstani citizens were able to buy land through the land auctions), the public mood was seemingly settled on the narrative which had spread through social media that the changes to the code allowed foreigners to buy up Kazakh land. Besides, the issue of land had become a lightning rod for wider material concerns regarding the economic conditions in the country. Declining economic growth was now unmasking long-standing frustrations among the population (Inosmi, 2016).

The government, police and security services' response to the protests was heavy-handed as hundreds of activists and journalists were arrested, detained and fined for public disturbance. Attempts to organise large-scale protests throughout the country on May 21st were thwarted by the authorities arresting activists and independent journalists in advance and by restricting the use of social media by blocking Facebook, Vkontakte, Twitter and Instagram alongside the Viber and WhatsApp messaging services (Radio Azattyk, 2016).

The regime's response to opposition voice appearing in this way was twofold. Firstly, sanctions of arrest, trial and imprisonment were placed against the most vocal and prominent protestors, activists, and independent journalists with at least forty-four people reported as being arrested (Baydalinova, 2016). While some were released and fined after a short duration, others faced lengthy spells behind bars such as Maks Boqaev and Talghat Ayan who were both sentenced to 5 years imprisonment for their part in the protests.

The government also responded with a media campaign claiming the protests were an attempt to overthrow the government and laid the blame of an attempted coup-d'état on an otherwise relatively obscure businessman, Tokhtar Tuleshov, who was already in prison awaiting trial on corruption charges (Lillis, 2016a, 2016b). Secondly, the government also responded through efforts of institutional adaptation. Initially, a moratorium was placed on reform of the land code, the agriculture minister was dismissed, and a Ministry of Information and Communication was formed to better inform the public about future policy changes (one of the perceived deficiencies of the government was that considerable misinformation about the revisions to the land code was able to spread so rapidly and so far without effective rebuttal) (Regnum, 2016). Then, when further unrest ensued, the president announced the creation of a land commission which would travel the country speaking to key stakeholders in the agricultural sector to determine how to proceed with the revisions to the land code and for future investment needs in the sector without resorting to the privatisation of land (Sholk, 2016). Finally, in August, in a rare public backdown, the president announced the initial moratorium on the land code would be extended for five years while the land commission undertook further work (Turebekova, 2016).

The land protests of 2016 in Kazakhstan can explain how sanctions and institutional adaptation can have a paradoxical effect. Sanctions and institutional adaptation strengthen the regime against internal threats in immediate response to the emergence of grassroots opposition voice, but in tightening the public space through coercive measures, as well as taking the issue back under state control (e.g., the land commission in this case), such strategies only serve to potentially create more discontent in the future. The land protests are an example of this, given the way the government was taken by surprise at their outbreak and as there was no feedback signal previously which prefigured their occurrence.

2019 Election Protests

On 19 March 2019 after nearly 30 years in power Nursultan Nazarbayev resigned as the president of Kazakhstan. As Chairman of the Senate, the upper chamber of parliament, Kassym-Zhomart Tokayev ascended the presidency according to the constitution. Nazarbayev's age and his aim to shape his own legacy while still alive were possibly the key motivating factors for his surprise announcement. Half of Kazakhstan's population is under the age of 30 and Nazarbayev's decision to resign represented a 'transformational moment' for the so-called 'Nazarbayev Generation'

(Laruelle, 2019, 2).[8] Nazarbayev's resignation resulted in the opening of public space for the political 'voice' of this younger generation. This voice emerged, however, largely in response to the immediate decisions taken by Nazarbayev's successor once he had sworn the oath of the presidency. In the constitutional and ceremonial handover of power in the *Mazhilis*, Tokayev praised Nazarbayev and awarded the outgoing president with the special honorary titles of 'Khalyk Karagarmany' (national hero) and 'Altyn Zhuldyz' (hero of labour), announced the renaming of the capital Astana to Nur-Sultan (after Nazarbayev) and appointed Nazarbayev's daughter, Dariga, as the Chair of the Senate (upper legislative chamber). These first decisions by the new president were an indicator that the ex-president would continue to maintain power and influence over Tokayev.[9] The renaming of the Capital attracted considerable ridicule and was understood as another component of the Nazarbayev personality cult (Auespekova, 2020; Village, 2019). In the weeks following Nazarbayev's resignation Tokayev announced there would be a pre-term presidential election—a way for him to obtain his own electoral mandate. Nazarbayev's resignation, the election, and the raft of personalised policies, such as the renaming of the capital, became the spark for an outburst of non-oligarchic public voice, predominantly from the youth of Kazakhstan.

This youth public voice took form in both individual and group oppositional acts. But the protests were grassroots-based and largely spontaneous, and again, caught the regime off guard. Individual actions often took the form of an art protest. Soon after Nazarbayev's resignation, a then 18-year-old Almaty-based artist, Medina Bazargali, went viral on social media, when she filmed herself walking around the city in a state of part-distress, part-delirium and part-liberation, repeating 'Nursultan in not my city, Tokayev is not my president, Dariga is not my speaker of the Senate, I have a choice'. Noted by some analysts as a 'performance',[10] Bazargali's mantra became the chief clarion call for protests which ran

---

[8] Author's interview with Almaty youth, 16 May 2019, Almaty Kazakhstan. Many similar sentiments were echoed by informal conversations with Almaty Youth during May 2019 while on fieldwork in Kazakhstan.

[9] Despite resigning from the presidency, Nazarbayev continued to hold the title of *Elbasi*, leader of the nation, remained head of the *Nur Otan* (Light of Fatherland) party, and as lifelong head of the National Security Council.

[10] Author's interview with Edil Basialov, 25 March 2019, Bishkek, Kyrgyzstan.

through the spring in the run-up to the election (Radio Azattyk, 2019a). Further unsanctioned protests followed Bazargali's 'performance'. For example, during the Almaty marathon in April, two young protestors, Asya Tulesova and Beibarys Tolymbekov, unfolded a banner stating: 'You cannot run from the truth,' and underneath the hashtags #Adil-SailayUshin ("For Fair Elections") in Kazakh and #YMenyaestVybor ("I Have a Choice") in Russian. Tulesova and Tolymbekov, were arrested and sentenced to fifteen days in prison for 'disturbing the holding of peaceful assemblies' and for holding an unsanctioned protest. Further small individual examples of public voice followed. For instance, Almaty-based artist Roman Zakharov hung a banner from an Almaty overpass citing the Kazakhstani constitution that 'the only source of the state power is the people'. He was arrested, charged and found guilty of littering (Vlast, 2019). In Uralsk in Northwestern Kazakhstan, video-blogger Aslan Sagutdinov undertook a one-man 'ironic' protest by holding up a blank banner. He was arrested by the police, even when his placard was empty of words and when he expressed no overtly political statements.

Larger group-based rallies followed on from these more individualistic ad-hoc protests. Large-scale anti-government protests took place in Almaty and Nur-Sultan on 1st May. They had been called for by the exiled Mukhtar Ablyazov (see previous chapter). Hundreds were arrested (Radio Azattyk, 2019b). Further protests calling for fair elections and political reform took place on election day on June 9th and later on July 6th on the 'Day of the Capital',[11] September 21st, October 26th and November 9th (Asylbek, 2019). In each case, many were arrested. While these protests nominally featured members of Ablyazov's banned Democratic Choice of Kazakhstan, they also included a new organisation, *Oyan, Kazakhstan* (Wake Up Kazakhstan) created by this youth generation who had found themselves politicised and prepared to activate their voice in the aftermath of Nazarbayev's resignation. *Oyan, Kazakhstan* describes itself as a civil movement with a political agenda.[12] The movement participated in many of the protests through 2019, but also undertook their own events including #sereun (translates as walk), which was aimed for people to get "acquainted, establish an open dialogue, and "return" public places to independent citizens of Kazakhstan... for young people to exchange

---

[11] The Day of the Capital public holiday also coincides with Nazarbayev's birthday.
[12] Author's interview with member of *Oyan, Kazakhstan* via Skype, 14 August 2019.

opinions on various topics' (Radio Azattyk, 2019c). These open-air public meet ups were one way of getting round the protest laws as they included music and poetry performances—and the group streamed them live on Facebook, Instagram and other social media platforms.

The protests which took place in 2019 were varied, widespread and, for Kazakhstan, large in number. While many were associated with the elections and concerned claims being made on the government for genuine political reform, others centred on different issues. For example, as noted earlier in the chapter, prior to Nazarbayev's resignation a group of mothers had protested in Astana in response to an apartment fire which had killed a young family, demanding greater social support for needy families (Zhoyamergen, 2019), while in March protests took place against the renaming of the Capital to Nur-Sultan (Radio Azattyk, 2019d). What the protests of 2019 illustrate is the heterogenous nature of grassroots opposition and the varied nature of this public voice. There are individual-level protests, small art-based 'performative' protests, new civic organisations (*Oyan, Kazakhstan*) and older political groupings linked to one of Kazakhstan's most well-known oligarchs. The nature of claims is also varied. While the political mobilisation pertaining to Zhanaozen and the land protests centred largely on material issues related to socio-economic concerns, the election protests tended towards more ideational issues—political rights, political reform, and fair and free elections. Some involved in protests have alluded to the distinction between ideational and material claims as one which is also a class and language divide between the more rural and Kazakh-speaking parts of the population and the more urban and Russian-speaking population. As noted by one member of *Oyan, Kazakhstan*:

> When they (broader people, Kazakh-speaking population) people think about *Oyan, Kazakhstan*, they call us hipsters, who were educated abroad, who sit around drinking coffee, and the truth is there is not a lot of support from the Kazakh-speaking population. They have different triggers they are really concerned with the issue of land. You can talk to them if it is about the issue of Russia or China taking land.[13]

These disparate forms of public voice with their varied claims on government are difficult for the regime to grasp as a totality. There is not a

---

[13] Author's interview with member of *Oyan, Kazakhstan*, via Skype, 15 August 2019.

clear coordinated and specific response that the regime can unleash on a targeted opposition in the same way that it is possible with institutional opposition and the oligarchic voice we saw in the previous chapter. Like with the Zhanaozen and land protests, the approach from the regime is scattergun and largely ineffective at controlling the threat to regime stability. The authorities acted as expected in terms of illegal protests—by way of individual sanctions. Protestors found themselves arrested and in some cases with short prison sentences, although most received administrative fines (Sansei, 2019). Similar to the land protests of 2016, the regime also sought to see off potential protests by shutting down the Internet making it difficult for any form of coordinated or planned protest. This was what played out on the 9 May when Mukhtar Ablyazov had called for simultaneous rallies in Almaty and Nur-Sultan. The regime closed off several social media sites (e.g., Facebook, Instagram, Telegram, YouTube) while also blocking key independent news websites (e.g., *Vlast*, *Azattyk*, *The Village*, *Ak Zhaiyk* among many others) and detained suspected protestors in advance (Radio Azattyk, 2019e).

Sanctions, however, were never going to be enough. The regime did opt for a form of institutional adaptation, but its effectiveness and the extent to which the regime was observed as meeting or addressing its perceived deficiencies was limited. In the aftermath of the presidential election in June, and the protests and rallies which accompanied the vote, the new president, Tokayev, announced the creation of the National Council of Public Trust (NCPT). The NCPT is a consultative and advisory body whose main aim is 'to develop proposals and recommendations on topical issues of state policy based on a broad discussion with representatives of the public, political parties, and civil society' (Forbes, 2019). The composition of the body did feature prominent voices within broader Kazakh civil society, including some of those involved in the earlier iteration of institutional opposition such as former Deputy Prime Minister and co-leader of *Ak Zhol* and *Nagyz Ak Zhol* opposition parties from the 2000s, Oraz Zhandosov, and Assylbek Kozhakhmetov who had previously been the leader of the Ablyazov-funded *Alga* opposition party. To some extent, the establishment of the NCPT was an attempt by the regime to put in place a feedback signal with broader society—something that had been absent since the marginalisation of institutional opposition. Nonetheless, the larger point regarding the NCPT was that it was part of a broader strategy of Tokayev to be seen as responsive to the grassroots opposition concerns regarding political reform. Tokayev went on to announce the concept of the 'listening state' which according to Tokayev 'promptly and effectively responds to all constructive requests from citizens' (Smaiyl, 2019). The 'listening state' concept and the NCPT have been largely viewed as declarative—with even some members of the newly established body quitting, expressing dissatisfaction with the work of the body (Doszhanov, 2020). Tokayev also sought to act on a promise made during the election campaign to begin the process of political reform in Kazakhstan. This appeared initially in the revised law on public assemblies discussed earlier in the chapter which ostensibly was intended to make it easier to organise public protests (Rittmann, 2020). The revised law did little to change the control authorities have over who and where groups and individuals can hold public protests (Pannier, 2020). Other elements of Tokayev's political reform agenda were also revealed to be shallow. An attempt to increase political competition only went as far as decreasing the number of members required to register a political party from 40,000 to 20,000, and a 30% quota for women and youth on party lists. Such incremental changes did little to change the broad discretion that the regime had in controlling the types of organisations which could be registered as political parties (Alzhanov, 2020). All registered political parties in Kazakhstan remained largely pro-regime.

These efforts of institutional adaptation perceptibly were an attempt at the regime wanting to provide the impression of reacting and 'listening' to the concerns raised by protestors in 2019. As noted by the former prominent opposition activist, Petr Svoik, such democratic reforms in Kazakhstan 'adopted by the regime are a decoration of external forms without deep content. It is more imitative than a real system and it is built very reliably, but too primitive'.[14] As such, the concept of the 'listening state' and the associated reform were not significant enough changes to satisfy the on-going grassroots-based opposition which had emerged in the previous decade in Kazakhstan. The regime was accused of 'listening, but not hearing' (Radionov, 2020). Neither the material nor ideational concerns which had given rise to a persistent use of non-oligarchic public voice, and which had generated a grassroots and often spontaneous opposition in Kazakhstan, had been addressed. While socio-economic and political claims would subside under the weight of the Covid-19 pandemic, it was only to be a matter of time before they

---

[14] Author's interview with Petr Svoik, 11 May 2019, Almaty, Kazakhstan.

surfaced again. Without a reliable feedback signal the regime in Kazakhstan continued to have little warning of when the next 'shock' to its stability would come from, and from where.

2022 *Qandy Qantar (Bloody January)*

When the 'shock' did arrive, it came at the regime from nowhere and was more violent, bloody and critical to regime stability than ever before. The events of January 2022 in Kazakhstan are too close to offer a full and deeply considered analysis. At the time of writing, we are still less than two months from the violence and bloodshed which took place. As noted above, none of the examples discussed in this chapter of the essay are intended to provide comprehensive accounts of these forms of mobilisation and political voice, and none is more the case than with the events of January 2022 given how recently the protests took place. Rather, the point remains to demonstrate the emergence and nature of non-oligarchic public voice outside the regime (as per nodal point four in the opposition agency matrix in authoritarian systems, see Chapter 2), and the analytical value of using Hirschman's exit, voice and loyalty frame to understand political opposition in authoritarian systems.

The events of 2022 began in Western Zhanaozen on January 2 when planned rises to the price of liquified petroleum gas (LPG) came into force leading to protests against the doubling of the cost of LPG.[15] In the next two days protests spread across the whole country, but the focus of the rallies shifted beyond just dissatisfaction with the regime's hike in the price of LPG. In Almaty, the heterogenous nature of grass-roots opposition saw a range of interests come out into the streets on January 4. *Oyan, Kazakhstan,* nationalist groups, the unregistered Democratic Party of Kazakhstan, led by former journalist Zhanbolat Mamay and many others not affiliated with any specific political or civic organisation (such as unemployed youth and urban migrants) all participated at various rallies in Almaty during the day, meeting and joining at various points (Mazorenko & Kaisar, 2022). The protests encompassed wider socio-economic and political demands beyond the rise in LPG prices and thousands of people were drawn on to the streets across the whole country. These represented the built-up frustrations of a population which

---

[15] The cost of LPG went from 60 tenge per litre ($0.14) to 120 tenge ($0.28).

had been left behind by an unresponsive regime (Zhandayeva & Zhanmukanova, 2022). The protests across the country now became a call for justice, a better life and most significantly an end to the Nazarbayev regime.[16] People had grown tired of the ways in which the elites had stolen from them and grown rich while ordinary people struggled in their everyday lives (Mazorenko & Kaisar, 2022). The protests of January 4 in Almaty were peaceful, exuberant and civil, but the following day they took a violent turn. While the police and security services had sought to hold back the protestors, the crowd resisted and kept returning to the main square after being dispersed. On the 5 January the crowd in Almaty eventually seized the city administration building, but the events turned violent towards the evening as armed gangs of men began to dominate over peaceful protestors, looting began to take place, the police and security services melted away and armed riots took place, people were killed and the city burned. The airport and other important buildings in the city were taken over by armed groups. Violence also took place in other cities in the country.

Tokayev blamed the violence and uprising on 20,000 terrorists and bandits. He placed the whole of Kazakhstan in a state of emergency, the internet was blocked throughout the country and the president called in the services of the Collective Security Treaty Organisation (CSTO)[17] to protect key infrastructure in the country. Tokayev sacked the whole government, placed Karim Masimov (a close ally of Nazarbayev), head of the KNB (security services), under arrest for treason—and criticised the agency for failing to tackle the issue of terrorism. Significantly, Tokayev announced that he was taking over as the head of the National Security Council; a position previously held by Nazarbayev—nominally for life. Over the next few days, the Kazakh military slowly regained control of Almaty—although gun fights took place throughout the city. Thousands of protestors were arrested, and many were killed. In a televised address on 7 January Tokayev announced that he had ordered the security forces

---

[16] Even though Nazarbayev had resigned in 2019, the feeling persisted in the country that the former president remained influential and a central figure in political decision-making, overshadowing his successor Tokayev.

[17] The CSTO is the Russian-led security organisation which features Russia, Kazakhstan, Belarus, Armenia, Kyrgyzstan and Tajikistan. In the 30 years since its inception, the CSTO had never deployed troops in any members state dealing with an internal conflict. The deployment of CSTO armed personnel in Kazakhstan was a first.

and the army 'to shoot to kill without warning' (Lillis, 2022). While order was gradually restored, Tokayev announced that the rise in LPG prices had been removed for six months.

The events of January 2022 are too complex and recent to make complete sense of here. Aside from the obvious human cost and tragedy of the events, there are three points we can take away from what happened when considering the opposition-regime equilibrium in the case of Kazakhstan. Firstly, the events represent the tragic culmination of the story of political opposition in Kazakhstan over the last 30 years. As the prominent human rights lawyer, Yevgeni Zhovtis argued, 'the system that Mr. Nazarbayev created for thirty years - such a centralized system with the cleansing of the political space, independent media, but with mild authoritarianism, with a balance between the elites and maintaining these checks and balances - has not justified itself' (Loginova, 2022). Ultimately, Zhovtis is arguing that the system did not justify itself because it produced considerable socio-economic inequality which established frustration in society with a perceived self-serving elite that got rich off the backs of the system Nazarbayev created. At the same time, clearing the political space of institutional opposition in the 1990s and oligarchic opposition in the 2000s meant there were no formal channels for this venting of this frustration. Treating the oligarchic opposition in Kazakhstan in an ambiguous way—by not bringing them into the policy and decision-making process and taking them seriously—but also marginalising and sanctioning them—forcing them to exit the country or system all together—meant important feedback loops which were important for regime stability disappeared.

Secondly, when the non-institutional, non-oligarchic opposition emerged from 2011 onwards it was heterogenous and spontaneous in nature. It was always difficult for the regime to take aim at. The regime's response could be characterised as whack-a-mole. So varied are the claims and demands being made regarding the deficiency of the regime and its policy outputs, especially in economic terms, but also ideationally in political and rights terms, that at any moment the regime may have felt that a certain set of claims were managed, put back in the box, another could emerge from elsewhere.

Thirdly, and most significantly, the 2022 *qandy qantar* protests did see the overthrow of part of the regime. As Yevgeni Zhovtis has also noted, the events marked the end of the 'Nazarbayev era in the form in which it once was' (Loginova, 2022). One fundamental element of the mosaic of the protests was their anti-Nazarbayev nature. A chief slogan of the protests was 'shal ket' (old man out). Signs of streets named after Nazarbayev were torn off and a statue of Nazarbayev was torn down in the town of Taldykorgan. People in the streets no longer wanted to see Nazarbayev in charge (Aptaev, 2022). Tokayev took up positions which Nazarbayev previously held including as head of the National Security Council, the 'lifetime' position Nazarbayev created for himself to maintain influence after he left office, leader of the *Nur Otan* party (Nazarbayev's party) and the chair of the Assembly of the Peoples of Kazakhstan. Legislation was also amended by the *Mazhilis* which removed from law the requirement that the government had to agree on foreign and domestic policy with Nazarbayev (Vaal, 2022). Further signs of de-Nazarbayevification can be seen in the renaming of Nazarbayev's party from *Nur Otan* to *Amanat* (legacy of ancestors). All these developments signified the waning influence of the former president institutionally.[18] Nazarbayev had not been publicly seen during the events of *qandy qantar* and had not released any statement. He finally appeared in a short and strange video on 18 January claiming that he was now a pensioner and fully supported Tokayev. Key allies and relatives of Nazarbayev were also removed from their posts by Tokayev (or left at their own accord), including Nazarbayev's nephews Samat Abish who was deputy head of the National Security Committee and Kairat Satybaldy, Nazarbayev's son-in-law Timur Kulibayev who left his position as head of the Atameken business union and two of Nazarbayev's other sons-in-law Dimash Dosanov and Kairat Sharipbayev, who were removed from their posts as chairmen of KazTransOil and QazaqGas, respectively (Kumenov, 2022). In February Tokayev also gave the government just two months to develop a plan to repatriate money held in offshore accounts—a clear aim at the wealth accumulated by Nazarbayev, his family and close associates over the last 30 years (IWPR, 2022).

Such moves by Tokayev fed speculation that the reason the peaceful protests turned violent, and that the police and security services melted away on the night of the 5 January, was because of orders from officials within the KNB close to Nazarbayev (especially Masimov and Abish) who were concerned about the increasing influence and growing power

---

[18] Tokayev had actually taken over the position as head of Nur Otan in November 2021, a small sign that there were already shifts occurring at the top which were only accelerated with the events of January 2022.

of Tokayev (Ashimbaev, 2022). The retribution that Tokayev met out to these figures serves to underline such speculation. Thus, what started out as peaceful protests against price rises to LPG, turned into broader protests against the regime which then turned into an attempt coup of one part of the regime over the other. Whatever the truth, the Nazarbayev era is over and what has happened since is demonstrative of the de-Nazarbayevification of the regime (Alimov, 2022). The Nazarbayev regime is done—at least in how we have always known it over the last thirty years. Of course, Tokayev was part of that regime—but what is clear is that what began in January 2022 in terms of popular pressure and protest against the regime and its failure to reform and provide economic security for people is not over. There is likely more to come.

Conclusion

Part of the regime did fall during *qandy qantar*—and it was Nazarbayev and his closest circle of elites who lost. But it was a fall of his own making. It was a fall which is explained by the mutually constituted relationship between opposition and regime in the country over the last 30 years. Opposition agency, opposition exit and voice, led to this point. The regime's suppression of institutional opposition in the 1990s, and its ambiguous treatment of oligarchic opposition, led to the closing down of important feedback signals the regime required to stabilise its position. Opposition exit and voice across the first three nodal points of the opposition-regime matrix (see Chapter 3) and the regime response via sanctions and institutional adaptation created the space within which non-oligarchic spontaneous grassroots voice was the only conduit through which complaints about policy and regime deficiencies could be adequately expressed. As this chapter has detailed, these forms of non-oligarchic grassroots voice appeared as a series of 'shocks' to the regime. But the regime response in each instance lacked direction and a coherent homogenous target. The heterogenous nature and varied claims held by grassroots opposition are difficult to manage and contain—and therefore this explains why the events of 2022 were such a critical shock to the regime.

The crumbling of part of the Nazarbayev regime (Nazarbayev and his closest circle) in January 2022 demonstrates how over 30-year period the logic of opposition agency (whether in institutional, oligarchic or grassroots form) and its mutually constitutive relationship with the regime has shaped the dynamics of regime stability. It demonstrates how in the case of Kazakhstan opposition agency has shaped regime outcomes.

REFERENCES

Alexander, C. (2018). Homeless in the homeland: Housing protests in Kazakhstan. *Critique of Anthropology, 38*(2), 204–220.

Al Jazeera. (2011, December 18). Deadly riots spread in Kazakhstan oil region. *Al Jazeera*. Accessed 6 Mar 2022. https://www.aljazeera.com/news/2011/12/18/deadly-riots-spread-in-kazakhstan-oil-region

Alimov, E. (2022, January 21). Simbolicheskaya denazarbaevizatsiya v obmen na poki? O sdelkakh, ustupkakh sud'be imperii Nazarbaevykh. *Radio Azattyk*. Accessed 6 Mar 2022. https://rus.azattyq.org/a/simvolicheskaya-denazarbaevizatsiya-v-obmen-na-pokoy/31664333.html

Alzhanov, D. (2020, May 26). Pustye reform Tokayeva. *Vlast*. Accessed 5 Mar 2022. https://vlast.kz/avtory/39813-pustye-reformy-tokaeva.html

Aptaev, B. (2022, January 24). Kazakhsta s'belacy. Kul't lichnosti Nursultana Nazarbayeva ne perezhil yanvar' 2022 goda. *Mediazona*. Accessed 6 Mar 2022. https://mediazona.ca/article/2022/01/24/elbasy

Ashimbaev, D. (2022, January 19). Zima Patriarcha. *Turan Press*. Accessed 6 Mar 2022. https://turanpress.kz/politika-i-vlast/zima-patriarkha-2

Asylbek, B. (2019, December 30). Lyudi ustali. Protesty v 2019 gody: prichiny i posledstviya. *Radio Azattyk*. Accessed 3 Mar 2022. https://rus.azattyq.org/a/kazakhstan-2019-year-protests-sauses-and-consequences/30351048.html

Auespekova, A. (2020, March 23). Ya prosto smirilsya: Chto dumayuot Kazakhstantsy o pereimenovanni Astany spustya god. *New Times*. Accessed 6 June 2020. https://newtimes.kz/obshchestvo/107303-ia-prosto-smirilsia-chto-dumaiut-kazakhstantsy-o-pereimenovanii-astany-spustia-god

Baydalinova, G. (2016, May 24). Kazakhstan: Protests lead to wave of arrests of journalists. *Reporters without borders*. Accessed 17 June 2016. https://rsf.org/en/news/kazakhstan-protests-lead-wave-arrests-journalists

Beisembayeva, D., Kolesova, E., & Papoutsaki, E. (2017). The Zhanaozen crisis and Oralmans' place in the (re) construction of Kazakh national identity. *New Zealand Journal of Asian Studies, 19*(2), 39–53.

Botaiuly, R. (2016, April 20). V Astane proshel odinochnyi piket za zemlyu. *Radio Azattyk*. Accessed 24 Feb 2022. https://rus.azattyq.org/a/27686363.html

Doszhanov, E. (2020, March 19). Mitingi i chrezvychaninye situatsii. Kakim byl pervyi god Tokayeva v Kazakhstane. *Nastoyashchee Vremya*. Accessed 14 Mar 2022. https://www.currenttime.tv/a/year-of-tokaev/30497260.html

Ferghana.ru. (2016, April 27). V Kazakhstane idut nescanktsionirovannye mitingi protiv prodazhi zemli, nesmotrya na raz'yasnenie. *Ferghana.ru*. Accessed 25 Feb 2022. https://www.fergananews.com/news/24706

Forbes. (2019, July 17). Kto voshyol v Natsional'nyi sovet obshchestvennogo doveriya pri prezidente Kazakhstana. *Forbes*. Accessed 6 Mar 2022. https://forbes.kz/process/kto_voshel_v_natsionalnyiy_sovet_obschestvennogo_doveriya_pri_prezidente_kazahstana/

Glushkova, S. (2011, August 8). Aktivist neftyanikov Natalya Sokolova osyzhdena na shest' let tyur'my. *Radio Azattyk*. Accessed online 24 Jan 2022. https://rus.azattyq.org/a/natalya_sokolova_oil_workers_lawyer_verdict/24290171.html

Human Rights Watch. (2012a, June 4). Kazakhstan: Oil workers convicted in flawed trial. *Human Rights Watch*. Accessed online 6 Mar 2022. https://www.hrw.org/news/2012a/06/04/kazakhstan-oil-workers-convicted-flawed-trial

Human Rights Watch. (2012b, October 9). Kazakhstan: Opposition leader jailed. *Human Rights Watch*. Accessed 6 Mar 2012b. https://www.hrw.org/news/2012a/10/09/kazakhstan-opposition-leader-jailed

Inosmi. (2016, May 6). Zemel'nye protesty otrazhenie nedovol'stva obshchim polozheniem del v strane? *Inosmi*. Accessed 25 Feb. https://inosmi.ru/20160506/236436458.html

IWRP. (2022, February 11). Nazarbayev's fading personality cult. *Institute for War and Peace Reporting*. Accessed 6 Mar 2022. https://iwpr.net/global-voices/kazakstan-nazarbayevs-fading-personality-cult

Jardine, B., Khashimov, S., Lemon, E., & Kyzy, A. (2021). *Mapping patterns of dissent in Eurasia: Introducing the Central Asia protest tracker*. Oxus Society for Central Asian Affairs.

Khamidov, A. (2011, August 22). Kazakhstan: Labor unrest denting Astana's economic image. *Eurasianet*. Accessed 24 Jan 2022. http://www.eurasianet.org/node/64077. Accessed 9 Sept 2014.

Koch, N. (2018). Disorder over the border: Spinning the spectre of instability through time and space in Central Asia. *Central Asian Survey, 37*(1), 13–30.

Kostyuchenko, E. (2011, December 20). Zhanaozen. *Novaya Gazeta*. Accessed 25 Jan 2022. https://novayagazeta.ru/articles/2011/12/20/47465-zhanaozen

Kudaibergenova, D. T. (2019). Compartmentalized ideology: Presidential addresses and Legitimation in Kazakhstan. In R. Isaacs & A. Frigerio (Eds.), *Theorizing Central Asian politics: The state, ideology and power* (pp. 145–166). Palgrave Macmillan.

Kumenov, A. (2021, February 23). Kazakhstan: Workers increasingly resorting to strikes, and succeeding. *Eurasianet*. Accessed 18 Jan 2022. https://eurasianet.org/kazakhstan-workers-increasingly-resorting-to-strikes-and-succeeding

Kumenov, A. (2022, January 17). Key Nazarbayev cronies undergo apparent purge. *Eurasianet*. Accessed 6 Mar 2022. https://eurasianet.org/kazakhstan-key-nazarbayev-cronies-undergo-apparent-purge

Lakhanuly, N. (2015, April 18). Intelligentsiya prizyvaet Nazarbayeva byt' ostorozhnym. *Radio Azattyk*. Accessed 20 Feb 2022. https://rus.azattyq.org/a/zemelniy-vopros-obraschenie-k-nazarbaevu/27680758.html

Laruelle, M. (2019). 'The Nazarbayev generation: A sociological portrait', lives'. In M. Laruelle (Ed.), *The Nazarbayev generation: Youth in Kazakhstan* (pp. 1–24). Rowman & Littlefield.

Lewis, D. (2016). Blogging Zhanaozen: Hegemonic discourse and authoritarian resilience in Kazakhstan. *Central Asian Survey, 35*(3), 421–438.

Lillis, J. (2011a, October 13). Kazakhstan: Labor dispute dragging energy production down. *Eurasianet*. Accessed 24 Jan 2022. https://eurasianet.org/kazakhstan-labor-dispute-dragging-energy-production-down

Lillis, J. (2011b, September 6). Kazakhstan: Astana confronts extremist threat. *Eurasianet*. Accessed 20 Jan 2022. https://eurasianet.org/kazakhstan-astana-confronts-extremist-threat

Lillis, J. (2012, April 23). Kazakhstan: Rights activists urge halt to Zhanaozen trial amid torture claims. *Eurasianet*. Accessed 30 Jan 2022. http://www.eurasianet.org/node/66032

Lillis, J. (2016a, May 24). Kazakhstan: Land issue fuelling social discontent. *Eurasianet*. Accessed 25 May 2016. https://eurasianet.org/kazakhstan-land-issue-fueling-social-discontent

Lillis, J. (2016b, June 1). Kazakhstan: Mud-slinging at protesters highlights apparent media double standards. *Eurasianet*. Accessed 3 June 2016. https://eurasianet.org/kazakhstan-mud-slinging-protesters-highlights-apparent-media-double-standards

Lillis, J. (2016c, June 6). Kazakhstan: Businessman accused of stoking land protests as coup plot. *Eurasianet*. Accessed 9 June 2016. https://eurasianet.org/kazakhstan-businessman-accused-stoking-land-protests-coup-plot

Lillis, J. (2019, January 21). Kazakhstan: The mothers that became the faces of dissent. *Eurasianet*. Accessed 31 Jan 2022. https://eurasianet.org/kazakhstan-the-mothers-that-became-the-faces-of-dissent

Lillis, J. (2022, January 7). Shoot to kill protesters, orders tough-talking Tokayev. *Eurasianet*. Accessed 5 Mar 2022. https://eurasianet.org/kazakhstan-shoot-to-kill-protesters-orders-tough-talking-tokayev

Loginova, O. (2022, January 10). Yevgenii Zhovtis, pravozashchitnik 'posle etikh sobytii budet soblazn v kakoi-to stepeni zakrychivat'. *Vlast.kz*. Accessed 5 Mar 2022. https://vlast.kz/politika/48096-evgenij-zovtis-pravozasitnik-posle-etih-sobytij-budet-soblazn-v-kakoj-to-stepeni-zakrucivat-gajki.html

Makhmutova, M., & Akhmetova, A. (2011). *Civil Society Index in Kazakhstan: CIVICUS Civil Society Index 2008–2010: Analytical country report*. Civicus.

Marat, E. (2016). Post-violence regime survival and expansion in Kazakhstan and Tajikistan. *Central Asian Survey, 35*(4), 531–548.

Mazorenko, D., & Kaisar, A. (2022, January 27). On the ground in Kazakhstan's protests: What really happened? *Open Democracy*. Accessed 5 Mar 2022. https://www.opendemocracy.net/en/odr/what-really-happened-kazakhstan-protests-january/

Mukhanov, B. (2018, March 13). Partiyu Ablayzova DVK priznali ekstremistskoi organizatsiei v Kazakhstane. *InformBuro*. Accessed 19 Jan 2022. https://informburo.kz/novosti/partiyu-ablyazova-dvk-priznali-ekstremistkoy-organizaciey-v-kazahstane-.html

Najibullah, F. (2019, February 12). Tragic fire in Astana gives Kazakh mothers' protests new momentum. *Radio Free Europe/Radio Liberty*. Accessed 19 Jan 2022. https://www.rferl.org/a/tragic-fire-in-astana-gives-kazakh-mothers-protests-new-momentum/29765930.html

Orazgaliyeva, M. (2016, June 9). Kazakh president declares June 9 as national day of mourning. *Astana Times*. Accessed 20 Jan 2022. https://astanatimes.com/2016/06/kazakh-president-declares-june-9-as-national-day-of-mourning/

Pannier, B. (2020, January 20). Kazakh officials force protesters into faraway places for opposition rallies. *Radio Free Europe/Radio Liberty*. Accessed 18 Jan 2022. https://www.rferl.org/a/kazakh-officials-force-protesters-into-faraway-places-for-opposition-rallies/30387955.html

Pirani, S. (2021, December 21). Who fired the shots? *The Ecologist*. Accessed online 24 January 2022. https://theecologist.org/2021/dec/16/who-fired-shots

Ponomarev, V. A. (1991). *Obshchestvennye organizatsii v Kazakhstane i Kyrgyzstane (1987–1991)*. Glagol.

Pron, E., & Szwajnoch, E. (2019, October 31). Kazakh anti-Chinese protests and the issue of Xinjiang detention camps. *The Central Asia-Caucasus Analyst*. Accessed 18 Jan 2022. http://www.cacianalyst.org/publications/analytical-articles/item/13593-kazakh-anti-chinese-protests-and-the-issue-of-xinjiang-detention-camps.html

Radio Azattyk. (2016, May 21). 21 Maya 2016a goda zaderzhaniya i blokirovki. *Radio Azattyk*. Accessed 23 May 2016. http://rus.azattyq.org/a/kazakhstan-mitingi-protesta-zemelnaya-reforma-azattyq/27748653.html

Radio Azattyk. (2019a, May 1). "Boikot i Narod ustal!" Nesanktsionirovannye aktsii I zaderzhaniya v Nur-Suttane i Almaty. *Radio Azattyk*. Accessed 7 June 2020. https://rus.azattyq.org/a/kazakhstan-nur-sultan-almaty-rally-1-may/29914075.html

Radio Azattyk. (2019b, May 2). Protesty 1 Maya. Ka keto bylo. *Radio Azattyk*. Accessed 3 Mar 2022. https://rus.azattyq.org/a/kazakhstan-1-may-protest/29915649.html

Radio Azattyk. (2019c, June 21). Dvuzhenie Oyan Kazakhstan provelo aktsiyu seruen v gorodakh Kazakhstana. *Radio Azattyk.* Accessed 7 June 2020. https://rus.azattyq.org/a/30012986.html

Radio Azattyk. (2019d, June 9). Massovye zaderzhaniya i soobshcheniya o narushcheniya v den' golosovaniya. *Radio Azattyk.* Accessed 6 Mar. https://rus.azattyq.org/a/kazakhstan-detentions-presidential-election-9-june/29989331.html

Radio Azattyk. (2019e, May 9). Den' pobedy nad zdravym smyslom. Blokirovki i zaderzhaniya 9 May. *Radio Azattyk.* Accessed 9 May 2019. https://rus.azattyq.org/a/kazakhstan-9-maya-blokirovki-zaderzhania/29930113.html

Radionov, V. (2020, December 25). Clyshayut, no ne slyshat. Yevgenii Zhovtis o glukhom gosudarstve. *Kz.media.* Accessed 5 Mar 2022. https://kz.media/archives/36985

Regnum. (2016, May 5). Nazarbaev otstupil: chinovniki budut cledit' za nastroeniyami v sotsetyakh. *Regnum.* Accessed 28 Dec 2018. https://regnum.ru/news/polit/2128839.html

Rittmann, M. (2020, May 28). Kazakhstan's 'reformed' protest law hardly an improvement. *Human Rights Watch.* Accessed 22 Jan 2022. https://www.hrw.org/news/2020/05/28/kazakhstans-reformed-protest-law-hardly-improvement

Rittmann, M. (2021, July 22). A sustained crackdown on independent worker organising—Kazakhstan, a case study. *The Foreign Policy Centre.* Accessed 30 Jan 2022. https://fpc.org.uk/a-sustained-crackdown-on-independent-worker-organising-kazakhstan-a-case-study/

Salmon, P. (2011). Repression intensifies against Kazakh oil workers' uprising. *Debatte: Journal of Contemporary Central and Eastern Europe, 19*(1–2), 507–510.

Salmon, P. (2012). Police Massacre has opened a dark chapter for Kazakh workers' movement. *Debatte: Journal of Contemporary Central and Eastern Europe, 20*(1), 73–77.

Sanghera, B., & Satybaldieva, E. (2021). *Rentier capitalism and its discontents: Power, morality and resistance in Central Asia.* Palgrave Macmillan.

Sansei, D. (2019, May 2). Chto stalo s zaderzhannymi i kto oni. *Radio Azattyk.* Accessed 6 Mar 2022. https://rus.azattyq.org/a/kazakhstan-what-happened-to-people-during-a-rally-on-may-1st/29917561.html

Satpayev, D., & Umbetaliyeva, T. (2015). The protests in Zhanaozen and the Kazakh oil sector: Conflicting interests in a Rentier State. *Journal of Eurasian Studies, 6*(2), 122–129.

Sholk, D. (2016, June 15). Kazakhstan's land reforms. *The Diplomat.* Accessed 20 June 2016. https://thediplomat.com/2016/06/kazakhstans-land-reforms/

Smaiyl, M. (2019, September 2). Tokaev o mitingakh: Nuzhno razreshat' i vydelyat' mesta ne na okraonakh. *Tengrinews*. Accessed 5 Mar 2022. https://tengrinews.kz/kazakhstan_news/tokaev-mitingah-nujno-razreshat-vyidelyat-mesta-na-okrainah-378015/

Socialism.kz.info. (2011, May 30). Press-reliz aktivistov profsoyuza 'Karazhanbasmunai' po fakty aresta Natal'i Sokolovoi i presledovaniya bastyushchikh neftyanikov. *Socialism.kz.info*. Accessed 12 Feb 2022. http://socialismkz.info/?p=2206

Toguzbaev, K. (2011, December 22). Nazarbayev v Zhanaozene. *Radio Azattyk*. Accessed 30 Jan 2022. https://rus.azattyq.org/a/nursultan_nazarbaev_unrest_in_mangistau_province/24430106.html

Toguzbaev, K. (2018, June 13). Shanyrak 12 let spustya. Sobytiya, o kotorykh zabyvayut? *Radio Azattyk*. Accessed 18 Jan 2022. https://rus.azattyq.org/a/shanyrakskiye-sobytia-12-let-spustya/29356950.html

Toiken, S. (2016, April 14). Protest v Atyray protiv prodazhi zemli. *Radio Azattyk*. Accessed 24 Feb 2022. https://rus.azattyq.org/a/protest-v-atyrau-protiv-prodazhi-zemel-inostrantsam/27693602.html

Toleukhanova, A. (2016a, September 20). Kazakhstan: Mortgage rallies continue despite protest fears. *Eurasianet*. Accessed online 18 Jan 2022. https://eurasianet.org/kazakhstan-mortgage-rallies-continue-despite-protest-fears

Toleukhanova, A. (2016b, May 6). Zemel'ne protesty – otrazhenie nedovol'stva obshchim polozheniem del v strane? *Eurasianet*. Accessed 20 Feb 2022. https://inosmi.ru/2016c0506/236436458.html

Totaro, M., & Sorbello, P. (2021). Oil, capital and labour around the caspian. In R. Isaacs & E. Marat (Eds.), *The Routledge handbook of contemporary Central Asia*. Routledge.

Trotsenko, P. (2017, January 23). Neudobnaya profsoyuznaya organizatsiya. *Radio Azattyk*. Accessed 30 Jan 2022. https://rus.azattyq.org/a/neudobnaya-profsouznaya-organyzacia/28251081.html

Turebekova, A. (2016, August 23). Kazakhstan extends by five years moratorium on controversial land code amendments. *The Astana Times*. Accessed 28 Dec 2016. https://astanatimes.com/2016/08/kazakhstan-extends-by-five-years-moratorium-on-controversial-land-code-amendments/

Vaal, T. (2022, January 27). S Nazarbayevym bolshe ne budut soglasovuvat' initsiativy po vnutrennei i vneshnei politike. *Vlast*. Accessed 6 Mar 2022. https://vlast.kz/novosti/48393-s-nazarbaevym-bolse-ne-budut-soglasovyvat-iniciativy-po-vnutrennej-i-vnesnej-politike.html

The Village. (2019, March 25). Eto imya dal mne dedushka v chest' sami znaete kogo: Nursultan yob imeni Astane i president. *The Village*. Accessed 6 June 2020. https://www.the-village.kz/village/people/people/5229-menya-zovut-nursultan

Vlast. (2019, April 29). Pyat' sutok aresta dali eshchyo odnomu almatintsu za plakat. *Vlast*. Accessed 6 Mar 2022. https://vlast.kz/novosti/32961-pat-sutok-aresta-dali-ese-odnomu-almatincu-za-plakat.html

Yanovskaya, M., & Kislov, D. (2012, December 16). God posle Zhanaozena. Sudy nespravedlivy, oppozitsiya obezglavlena, repressii usilivayutsya. *Ferghana.ru*. Accessed 25 Jan 2022. https://www.fergananews.com/articles/7571

Yessenova, S. (2010). Borrowed places: Eviction wars and property rights formalization in Kazakhstan. In D. C. Wood (Ed.), *Economic action in theory and practice: Anthropological investigations* (pp. 11–45). Research in Economic Anthropology, Vol. 30. Emerald Group Publishing Limited.

Ziegler, C. E. (2010). Civil society, political stability, and state power in Central Asia: Cooperation and contestation. *Democratization, 17*(5), 795–825.

Zhandayeva, R., and Zhanmukanova, A. (2022, January 10). Kazakhstan's instability has been building for years. *Foreign Policy*. Accessed online 5 Mar 2022. https://foreignpolicy.com/2022/01/10/kazakhstan-instability-protests-nazarbayev/

Zhoyamergen, O. (2019, February 6). Posobiya, zhil'e, otstavka ministra. Mnogodetnye ozvuchili trebovaniya. *Radio Azattyk*. Accessed 3 Mar 2022. https://rus.azattyq.org/a/kazakhstan-astana-mothers-with-many-children/29754282.html

CHAPTER 7

Conclusion

What does the story of opposition-regime relations in Kazakhstan over the last thirty years tell us about the logic and dynamics of opposition in authoritarian regimes in general? There are always limits to the extent we can generalise from any given case, and this is ultimately an interpretative essay, and as such this study is no different in terms of its limitations in this respect. However, there are several aspects of the Kazakhstani case which do illuminate our understanding and appreciation for political opposition agency in authoritarian systems.

OPPOSITION IN AUTHORITARIAN SYSTEMS

Returning to Chapter 2, the example of Kazakhstan has highlighted the importance of moving beyond institutional definitions of opposition in authoritarian systems. It is commonplace in the scholarly literature on opposition in authoritarian regimes to view the opposition through the lens of their institutional manifestation, namely political parties, while continuing to characterise them via the systemic versus non-systemic dichotomy (Armstrong et al., 2020; Buckles, 2019; Selçuk & Hekimci, 2020). While some scholars have sought to branch out from the institutional definition of opposition in authoritarian contexts, such efforts have remained limited (Bedford & Vinatier, 2019). Here the case of

© The Author(s), under exclusive license to Springer Nature Switzerland AG 2022
R. Isaacs, *Political Opposition in Authoritarianism*, The Theories, Concepts and Practices of Democracy, https://doi.org/10.1007/978-3-031-06536-1_7

Kazakhstan has highlighted that to understand the logic of opposition in authoritarian contexts we need to break more clearly from viewing opposition within the traditional parameters of being restricted to political parties. The threefold typology of opposition in authoritarian systems (individual, organisational and grassroots) discussed in Chapter 1 was an effort to capture the potential variety. For instance, when we reflect on the story of political opposition in Kazakhstan over the last thirty years, while institutional opposition has performed a role, especially in the first decade of Kazakhstan's independence, other forms of opposition have been equally if not more so important. The oligarchic opposition, for example, while often using political parties as platforms, was also more centred on a specific individual, their wealth and personal networks. Thus, opposition can be centred on the individual—whether elite or non-elite (as the examples of individual acts of opposition in Chapter 6 allude to). Even when considering organisational forms of opposition, the case of Kazakhstan demonstrates a variety beyond just political parties. While Chapters 4 and 5 highlighted the importance of political parties to opposition agency in Kazakhstan, Chapter 6 also demonstrated other organisational forms, especially trade unions (in relation to the Zhanaozen protests) and to some extent *Oyan, Kazakhstan*. They are organisational forms as they possess a semblance of a coordinated organisational structure and resources for mobilisation. At the same time, as the different examples of non-oligarchic and non-institutional forms of opposition presented in Chapter 6 show, opposition can emerge powerfully, and critically for the regime, in spontaneous, uncoordinated, and non-organisational forms through grassroots collective action. The general point is that the case of Kazakhstan has demonstrated that opposition in authoritarian contexts can contain multitudes.

None of this is to say that institutional opposition in authoritarian systems is not important. Evidently it is. But if we only focus on institutional opposition, we only get to see half the story. And, if we wish to understand the logic and dynamism of opposition in authoritarian spaces, and its potential as an agent and catalyst for change, then we need to know the full story of opposition, as much as that is possible. In Kazakhstan a focus on institutional opposition (and attempts to re-establish institutional opposition through oligarchic opposition) ends the story in 2013 when Bolat Abilov retires from the political scene. Capturing the grassroots opposition as a form of political opposition to the regime allowed us to read the full story of opposition and the importance of opposition agency for shaping regime outcomes, particularly in the case of Kazakhstan regime instability. In the case of Kazakhstan, this broader and more inclusive conceptualisation of opposition through the threefold typology of individual, organisational and grassroots opposition allows us to view a direct relationship between the foreclosing of institutional opposition in the 1990s to the events of *qandy qantar* in January 2022 which, in many respects, saw the decommissioning of the Nazarbayev regime.

Understanding Opposition-Regime Dynamics in Authoritarian Systems

A more complete story of political opposition also provides for a new perspective on opposition-regime equilibria in authoritarian systems. As noted in Chapter 2, there are generally two approaches to understanding regime-opposition equilibria in authoritarian systems. The first concerns the relationship between repression and dissent, and the second is centred on how the regime co-opts opposition elites offering resources and positions in exchange for loyalty, but the regime only does so when it considers the opposition a *credible* threat. The case of Kazakhstan, as analysed in this essay, departs from this literature because the regime's approach to opposition in Kazakhstan has been ambiguous in terms of the extent to which it viewed the opposition as a threat. The literature would suggest that if the regime sees the opposition as credibly engendering wider social protest or an elite-led coup-d'état then co-optation is required to ensure regime stability (Gandhi & Buckles, 2016; Magaloni, 2008). Kazakhstan is a curious case in this respect. Institutional opposition was foreclosed in the 1990s through the centralisation of power in the executive and the emergence of a personalised regime where economic spoils were fought over by competing elite groups with the president as the supreme arbiter of such disputes. In such a context, the opposition which emerged was oligarchic. Once such oligarchic opposition emerged Nazarbayev was left with the dilemma to co-opt or not. On the one hand, widespread co-optation of those elites associated with former Prime Minister Kazhegeldin or the DVK grouping (see Chapter 5) did not take place. On the other hand, the emergence of such opposition did appear to threaten regime stability, as the oligarchic opposition was perceived to be credible enough a threat to engender wider protest or a potential coup-d'état. Thus, heavy coercion and considerable institutional adaptation was undertaken to marginalise and neutralise the perceived threat to the regime through various sanctions (individual and organisational) and changes to the institutional architecture of the political environment (e.g., Law on Political Parties, changes to the electoral law, etc.). If the opposition is not perceived as a credible enough threat to the regime as to challenge the incumbent leadership's position, why go to such lengths to sanction and adapt the institutional architecture of the political space to remove them from the political scene? Ultimately, this was an ambiguous reading of the oligarchic opposition as with regard to its credible potency to destabilise the regime. The impact of this ambiguity, as the Kazakhstani case illustrates, is that the regime can act in an erratic way, unsure of where and to whom to direct sanctions towards, in the end applying them to a range of actors, some associated with grassroots opposition and others not.

Exit, Voice, Loyalty, Sanctions

As the introduction to this essay argued, one aim of this work was to concentrate on the agency of political opposition in authoritarianism and to analyse its impact on regime outcomes, all the while recognising the pre-eminence of regime agency in respect of regime-opposition relations. Hirschman's frame of exit, voice and loyalty was used to conceptualise and analyse opposition agency. As Chapter 3 highlighted, the case of oligarchic opposition in Kazakhstan contributes to already existing examples of the use of the exit, voice and loyalty frame to understand opposition agency vis-à-vis the regime. Like those studies, the Kazakhstani case only serves to complicate the simplicity of the dichotomy between exit and voice and illustrate its dynamic nature (Dowding et al., 2000; Pfaff & Kim, 2003). The choice and path of opposition agency between exit and voice is not a linear one. As Chapter 5 demonstrated with the analysis of the oligarchic opposition in Kazakhstan, opposition elites had various nodal points to move through in terms of the choices available to them between exit, voice and loyalty. Exit and voice is not a simple dichotomy. Exit comes in different forms and so does voice—and there are different combinations between them. In the case of Kazakhstan, four nodal points were identified—private internal voice inside the regime, exit the regime with or without public voice, exit the country/political system with or without public voice and non-elite public voice outside the system. But perhaps the most significant contribution this study can make concerns the way in which we can think about how regime sanctions condition or moderate opposition agency of exit and voice. As we observed in Chapter 5 some opposition figures (and parties) moved back and forth across these nodal points because of sanctions or the expectations of sanctions. For example, Bolat Abilov, Oraz Zhandosov, and Alikhan Baimenov were all part of the DVK movement that exited the regime in 2001 and used public voice to raise concerns with the evolving authoritarian nature of the Nazarbayev regime and the distribution of resources which gave preference to close family members of the president. However, having seen how two of the main proponents of the DVK movement, Galymzhan Zhakiyanov and Mukhtar Ablyazov, found themselves subject to the harshest sanctions (criminal court proceedings and prison sentences), Abilov, Zhandosov and Baimenov then established *AK Zhol* to be more 'constructive' with the regime. Sanctions, therefore, played an important role in moderating the tone of voice towards the regime and alongside institutional adaptation shaped the decisions pertaining to exit and voice at the different nodal points for opposition elites. In the case of Abilov and Zhandosov they eventually took nodal point three and exited the political system because of persistent sanctions against them and their political party, and the adaptations to the institutional environment which meant realistic prospects of electoral success alluded them. Baimenov, on the other hand, chose loyalty and no voice, slowly edging back into the regime by 2011. Thus, the case of Kazakhstan demonstrates the way in which exit and voice as a form of opposition agency in authoritarian systems is not a straightforward binary choice, but instead a multifaceted, on-going dynamic process of decision-making which is also shaped by the response from the regime in terms of sanctions and institutional adaptation. The case of Kazakhstan at least illustrates that there is a dialectical quality to exit, voice and loyalty with sanctions as an intervening variable.

AUTHORITARIAN (IN)STABILITY

Using exit and voice as a conceptual frame to understand opposition agency allowed for a greater focus on authoritarian regime dynamics, both in terms of stability and instability. In the case of Kazakhstan, it has allowed us to trace how opposition agency (through exit and voice) has shaped regime responses (sanctions and institutional adaptation) which in turn have shaped regime outcomes (stability versus instability). Chapter 6, therefore, illustrated how nodal point four of the exit, voice, loyalty matrix could assist in explaining the increasing rise in social discontent in Kazakhstan since 2011 onwards—and how an authoritarian regime can find itself in a perpetual state of instability. In other words, the case of Kazakhstan illustrates how authoritarian regimes which treat an opposition threat as ambiguous (rather than taking opposition seriously and seeking co-optation) are likely to end up in a continuous state of instability because the feedback provided by opposition agency disappears leaving the regime susceptible to grassroots, spontaneous opposition. The foreclosing of both institutional and oligarchic opposition in Kazakhstan meant that important feedback signals diminished regarding regime deficiencies especially as it pertained to policy. It was then non-oligarchic grassroots opposition which appeared in its place. But it was an opposition that the regime had little foreknowledge to anticipate. The events in Zhanaozen, the land protests, the election protests and events of *qandy qantar* were all exemplary of this phenomenon. It placed the regime in a persistent state of instability, unaware of where and when the next 'shock' would appear. Kazakhstan, therefore, illustrates how a regime-opposition equilibrium can exist in a paradoxical state of being simultaneously stable and unstable. While sanctions and institutional adaptation were used to stabilise the regime against oligarchic opposition agency of exit and voice, it only did so in the short to medium term because it removed the feedback signal that opposition agency had provided. The events of *qandy qantar* demonstrate the consequence of this inbuilt instability, in that over time, with each 'shock' to the regime, the situation becomes more perilous. In January 2022 part of the Kazakh regime did collapse with those elites closest to Nazarbayev being pushed out. But public voice against the regime persists, especially in terms of economic claims from workers in the West of the country with strikes over low wages, poor working conditions and political repression continuing during February and March 2022 (Baunov, 2022). In March 2002, President Tokayev proposed a raft of political reforms to address the claims voiced by grassroots opposition during *qandy qantar*. These reforms include proposals to transition away from the 'super-presidency', to reduce the number of members required for a political party to register (from 20,000 to just 5000), and to reform the electoral system to include 30% of parliamentary deputies to be elected by single district mandates. However, the proposed reforms do not include the free democratic election of regional governors, a fundamental aim of *Oyan, Kazakhstan*, suggesting that grassroots opposition voice is not finished in this respect (Najibullah, 2022).

It is hard to say what this study of opposition agency via exit and voice tells us about authoritarian regime stability or instability in other states. Kazakhstan's closest comparators would be that of the other Central Asian republics, but each of those states has their own specific dynamics. Countries such as Turkmenistan and Uzbekistan quickly marginalised any institutional opposition in the aftermath of collapse of the Soviet Union (and in fact political opposition immediately exited the country and system altogether existing only in exile since then). Oligarchic opposition has not been a phenomenon in either country, although there are signs of small-scale grassroots opposition, even in Turkmenistan, especially in relation to economic claims in what is a fast-declining economic situation. Kyrgyzstan has always had a much more active and vibrant political opposition, which too has appeared in multiple forms, but has been largely grassroots based and succeed in turning over the regime three times in the last 15 years. In Tajikistan, any direct comparison to Kazakhstan in terms of political opposition is complicated by the experience of civil war in the 1990s and the fact that President Emomali Rahmon had to bring the opposition into the government as part of the peace agreement (this was the Islamic Renaissance Party of Tajikistan [IRPT]). However, by 2015 Rahmon crushed the IRPT by outlawing it as a terrorist organisation.

There are two important things we can take from the case of Kazakhstan in relation to opposition agency to the cases of other post-Soviet Central Asian states. Firstly, how the regime in Kazakhstan got locked into a mutually constitutive cycle of stability and instability because of opposition agency should be something of a warning to other authoritarian regimes in the region. Closing off feedback signals regarding broader public discontent through the removal of institutional and other high-level elite forms of opposition only serves to build up pressure in the system which will require releasing at some point. When and where such spikes in public discontent occur become a largely unknowable factor for the regime. Secondly, Kazakhstan, and to some extent the rest of the Central Asian republics, illustrates that contrary to a great deal of the existing scholarship on opposition in authoritarian regimes, political opposition in non-democratic contexts is not static but rather is a fluid and dynamic phenomenon (as a recent study on opposition in Yemen has demonstrated) (Heibach & Transfeld, 2018). Kazakhstan and the other Central Asian republics demonstrate that opposition in authoritarian systems evolves, changes and adapts in terms of both the use of their agency in relation to exit and voice and in terms of how the regime responds. The logic of opposition in authoritarianism is a live ongoing phenomenon, and even if it is seemingly lying still and quiet, and ostensibly beaten and repressed, underneath it breathes and waits.

References

Armstrong, D., Reuter, O., & Robertson, G. (2020). Getting the opposition together: Protest coordination in authoritarian regimes. *Post-Soviet Affairs, 36*(1), 1–19.

Baunov, P. (2022, February 6). Making sense of Kazakhstan's 'Bloody January'. *bne Intellinews*. Accessed 16 Mar 2022. https://www.intellinews.com/central-asia-blog-making-sense-of-kazakhstan-s-bloody-january-part-1-233840/?source=blogs

Bedford, S., & Vinatier, L. (2019). Resisting the irresistible: 'Failed Opposition' in Azerbaijan and Belarus revisited. *Government and Opposition, 54*(4), 686–714.

Buckles, G. (2019). Internal opposition dynamics and restraints on authoritarian control. *British Journal of Political Science, 49*(3), 883–900.

Dowding, K., John, P., Mergoupis, T., & Van Vugt, M. (2000). Exit, voice and loyalty: Analytic and empirical developments. *European Journal of Political Research, 37*(4), 469–495.

Gandhi, J., & Buckles, G. (2016, April 7–10). *Opposition unity and co-optation in hybrid regimes*. Paper Presented at the Annual Midwest Political Science Association Conference, Chicago, IL, pp. 1–33.

Heibach, J., & Transfeld, M. (2018). Opposition dynamism under authoritarianism: The case of Yemen, 1994–2011. *Democratization, 25*(4), 597–613.

Magaloni, B. (2008). Credible power-sharing and the longevity of authoritarian rule. *Comparative Political Studies, 41*(4/5), 715–741.

Magaloni, B., & Kricheli, R. (2010). Political order and one-party rule. *The Annual Review of Political Science, 13*, 123–143.

Najibullah, F. (2022, March 18). Kazakh president unlikely to give up real power despite pledging end to 'super-presidency'. *Radio Free Europe/Radio Liberty*. Accessed 18 Mar 2022. https://www.rferl.org/a/kazakhstan-toqaev-reforms-analysis/31759365.html

Pfaff, S., & Kim, H. (2003). Exit-voice dynamics in collective action: An analysis of emigration and protest in the East German revolution. *American Journal of Sociology, 109*(2), 401–444.

Selçuk, O., & Hekimci, D. (2020). The rise of the democracy—Authoritarianism cleavage and opposition coordination in Turkey (2014–2019). *Democratization, 27*(8), 1496–1514.

Glossary

Akim Local Governor
DVK *Demokraticheskii Vybor Kazakhstana* (Democratic Choice of Kazakhstan)
Mazhilis Kazakhstan's Parliament
Nur Otan Light of Fatherland
OSDP Obshchnatsional'noi sotsial-demokraticheskoi partii (All-National Social Democratic Party)
Otan Fatherland
Oyan, Kazakhstan (Wake Up Kazakhstan)
Qandy qantar Bloody January
RNPK *Respublikanskaia narodnaia partiia Kazakhstana* (Republican Peoples Party of Kazakhstan)
SNEK *Soyuz narodnoi edinstvo Kazakhstana* (Union of Peoples Unity of Kazakhstan)
Vlast Power (but has far wider connotations entailing the administration of the authorities and the president)

Bibliography

Abdil'din, S. (1993). *Stanovlenie Parlamentarizma v Kazakhstane*. Sekretariat Soveta MPA.

Abdirova, A. (2011, July 2). Posle ubiistva politseiskikh Temirskii raion vyglyadit prifrontovym. *Radio Azattyk*. Accessed 20 Jan 2022. https://rus.azattyq.org/a/shubarshi_aktobe_police_islam_policia/24253559.html

Aitkhozhin, K., & Buluktaev, Y. (2003). *Rol' Parlamenta v sisteme gosudarstvennoi vlasti*. Tsentr Analiza Obshchestvennykh Problem.

Akkuly, S. (2010, November 24). U Rakhat Alieva trebyut kompensatsiyu za repressii i stradaniya v tyur'me. *Radio Azattyk*. Accessed online 7 Jan 2022. https://rus.azattyq.org/a/afanasenko_officer_Kazakhstan_civill_action_rakhat_alyev_/2228151.html

Akkuly, S. (2011, April 9). Zakat Askara Kunaeva predveshal skoryi konets Kunavea-starshego. *Radio Azattyk*. Accessed online 16 Dec 2021. https://rus.azattyq.org/a/askar_kunaev_december_riot_kazakhstan_/3551546.html

Albertazzi, D. (2009). Reconciling 'voice' and 'exit': Swiss and Italian populists in power. *Politics, 29*(1), 1–10.

Albrecht, H. (2013). *Raging against the machine: Political opposition under authoritarianism in Egypt*. Syracuse University Press.

Albrecht, H. (2015). How can opposition support authoritarianism? Lessons from Egypt. *Democratization, 12*(30), 378–397.

Alexander, C. (2018). Homeless in the homeland: Housing protests in Kazakhstan. *Critique of Anthropology, 38*(2), 204–220.

Al Jazeera. (2011, December 18). Deadly riots spread in Kazakhstan oil region. *Al Jazeera*. Accessed 6 Mar 2022. https://www.aljazeera.com/news/2011/12/18/deadly-riots-spread-in-kazakhstan-oil-region

Alimov, E. (2022, January 21). Simbolicheskaya denazarbaevizatsiya v obmen na poki? O sdelkakh, ustupkakh sud'be imperii Nazarbaevykh. *Radio Azattyk*. Accessed 6 Mar 2022. https://rus.azattyq.org/a/simvolicheskaya-denazarbaevizatsiya-v-obmen-na-pokoy/31664333.html

Alzhanov, D. (2020, May 26). Pustye reform Tokayeva. *Vlast*. Accessed 5 Mar 2022. https://vlast.kz/avtory/39813-pustye-reformy-tokaeva.html

Amanzholova, D. (2009). *Na Izlome. Alash v ethnopoliticheskoi istorii Kazakhstana*. Izdatel'skii dom 'Taimas'.

Amrekulov, N. (2000). Zhuzy v sotsialno-politicheskoi zhizni Kazakhstana. *Tsentral'naia Aziia i Kavkaz, 3*(9), 131–146.

Armstrong, D., Reuter, O., & Robertson, G. (2020). Getting the opposition together: Protest coordination in authoritarian regimes. *Post-Soviet Affairs, 36*(1), 1–19.

Anderson, J. (1997). Constitutional development in Central Asia. *Central Asian Survey, 16*(3), 301–320.

Alzhanov, M. (2004, December 3). Politicheskaya 'bomba; Zamanbeka Nurkadilova. *Respublika*. Accessed 27 June 2008 http://www.iwww.kub.info/article.php?sid=5522

Aptaev, B. (2022, January 24). Kazakhsta s'belacy. Kul't lichnosti Nursultana Nazarbayeva ne perezhil yanvar' 2022 goda. *Mediazona*. Accessed 6 Mar 2022. https://mediazona.ca/article/2022/01/24/elbasy

Arendt, H. (1951). *The origins of totalitarianism*. Harcourt Press.

Armstrong, D., Reuter, O. J., & Robertson, G. B. (2020). Getting the opposition together: Protest coordination in authoritarian regimes. *Post-Soviet Affairs, 36*(1), 1–19.

Ash, K. (2015). The election trap: The cycle of post-electoral repression and opposition fragmentation in Lukashenko's Belarus. *Democratization, 22*(6), 1030–1053.

Ashimbaev, D. (2022, January 19). Zima Patriarcha. *Turan Press*. Accessed 6 Mar 2022. https://turanpress.kz/politika-i-vlast/zima-patriarkha-2

Asylbek, B. (2019, December 30). Lyudi ustali. Protesty v 2019 gody: prichiny i posledstviya. *Radio Azattyk*. Accessed 3 Mar 2022. https://rus.azattyq.org/a/kazakhstan-2019-year-protests-sauses-and-consequences/30351048.html

Auespekova, A. (2020, March 23). Ya prosto smirilsya: Chto dumayuot Kazakhstantsy o pereimenovanni Astany spustya god. *New Times*. Accessed 6 June 2020. https://newtimes.kz/obshchestvo/107303-ia-prosto-smirilsia-chto-dumaiut-kazakhstantsy-o-pereimenovanii-astany-spustia-god

Babak, V. (2005). Kazakhstan: How its multiparty system came into being. *Central Asia and the Caucasus, 32*(2), 1–14.

Baitov, R. (2006, September 22). Kak Zh Tuyakbai s prezidentom vstrechalsya. *Nomad*. Accessed 31 Mar 2016. http://www.nomad.su/?a=3-200609 220227

Baizakova, G. (2021, February 28). 32 goda nazad voznikloa zactavivshee zamolchat yadernyi polygon dvizhenie Nevada-Semei'. *Kazinform*. Accessed online 18 Dec 2021. https://www.inform.kz/ru/32-goda-nazad-vozniklo-zastavivshee-zamolchat-yadernyy-poligon-dvizhenie-nevada-semey_a3758590

Balgimbayev, B. (2013, August 31). Kazakhstanskaya model' demokratii: stanovlenie i spetsifika. *Mezhdunarodnaya Akademiia Informatizatsii*. Accessed 7 June 2014. http://academy.kz/ru/normativnye-akty/entry/kazakhstanskaya-model-demokratii-stanovlenie-i-spetsifika

Barker, R. (1971). Introduction. In R. Barker (Ed.), *Studies in opposition* (pp. 1–30). Palgrave Macmillan.

Barry, B. (1974). Review article: Exit, voice, and loyalty. *British Journal of Political Science, 1*(4).

Bashin, T., & Gandhi, J. (2013). Timing and targeting of state repression in authoritarian elections. *Electoral Studies, 32*, 620–631.

Baunov, P. (2022, February 6). Making sense of Kazakhstan's 'Bloody January'. *bne Intellinews*. Accessed 16 Mar 2022. https://www.intellinews.com/central-asia-blog-making-sense-of-kazakhstan-s-bloody-january-part-1-233840/?source=blogs

Baydalinova, G. (2016, May 24). Kazakhstan: Protests lead to wave of arrests of journalists. *Reporters without borders*. Accessed 17 June 2016. https://rsf.org/en/news/kazakhstan-protests-lead-wave-arrests-journalists

Bazhkenova, G. (2017, April 11). Bezoruzhnyi proletariat. *Radio Azattyk*. Accessed 21 Jan 2022. https://rus.azattyq.org/a/kazakhstan-blogistan-bazhkenova-profsoyuz/28420815.html

Bedford, S., & Vinatier, L. (2019). Resisting the irresistible: 'Failed opposition' in Azerbaijan and Belarus revisited. *Government and Opposition, 54*(4), 686–714.

Beisembayeva, D., Kolesova, E., & Papoutsaki, E. (2017). The Zhanaozen crisis and Oralmans' place in the (re)construction of Kazakh National identity. *New Zealand Journal of Asian Studies, 19*(2), 39–53.

Beissinger, M. (2009). Nationalism and the collapse of the Soviet Union. *Contemporary European History, 18*(3), 331–347.

Bennett, W., & Segerberg, A. (2012). The logic of connective action. *Information, Communication & Society, 15*(5), 739–768.

Blondel, J. (1997). Political opposition in the contemporary world. *Government and Opposition, 32*(2), 462–486.

Bode, N., & Makarychev, A. (2013). The new social media in Russia. *Problems of Post-Communism, 60*(2), 53–62.

Boix, C., & Svolik, M. (2013). The foundations of limited authoritarian government: Institutions, commitment, and power-sharing in dictatorships. *The Journal of Politics, 75*(2), 300–316.

Botaiuly, R. (2016, April 20). V Astane proshel odinochnyi piket za zemlyu. *Radio Azattyk*. Accessed 24 Feb 2022. https://rus.azattyq.org/a/27686363.html

Brack, N., & Weinblum, S. (2011). Political opposition: Towards a new research agenda. *Interdisciplinary Political Studies, 1*(1), 69–78.

Brownlee, J. (2007). *Authoritarianism in the age of democratisation*. Cambridge University Press.

Brubaker, R. (1990). Frontier theses: Exit, voice and loyalty in East Germany. *Migration World, 18*(3/4), 12–17.

Buckles, G. (2019). Internal opposition dynamics and restraints on authoritarian control. *British Journal of Political Science, 49*(3), 883–900.

Buluktaev, Y. O., D'yachenko, C. A., & Karmazina, L. I. (1998). *Politicheskie Partii Kazakhstana Spravochnik 1998*. IPK.

Bunce, V. (1999). *Subversive institutions: The design and the collapse of socialism and the state*. Cambridge University Press.

Burkhanov, K., Sultanov, B., & Ayagan, A. (2006). *Sovremennaia Politicheskaia Istoriia Kazakhstana*. Institut Istorii i etnologii im. Ch. Ch. Valikhanova.

Butterfield, J., & Sedaitis, J. (1991). The emergence of social movements in the Soviet Union. In J. Sedaitis & J. Butterfield (Eds.), *Perestroika from below social movements in the Soviet Union* (pp. 1–12). Westview Press.

Carey, S. (2006). The dynamic relationship between protest and repression. *Political Research Quarterly, 59*(1), 1–12.

Cavatorta, F. (2009). 'Divided they stand, divided they fail': Opposition politics in Morocco. *Democratization, 16*(1), 137–156.

Cavatorta, F. (2013). *Civil society activism under authoritarian rule: A comparative perspective*. Routledge.

Chebotarev, A. (2006, November 7). Politicheskii krizis oseni 2011 goda i ego posledstviya 5 let spustya. *Kub*. Accessed 14 Dec 2006. http://www.kub.info/article.php?sid=15070

Cheng, E. W., & Chan, W. (2017). Explaining spontaneous occupation: Antecedents, contingencies and spaces in the umbrella movement. *Social Movement Studies, 16*(2), 222–239.

Collins, K. (2006). *Clan politics and regime transition in Central Asia*. Cambridge University Press.

Conrad, C. (2011). Constrained concessions: Beneficent dictatorial responses to the domestic political opposition. *International Studies Quarterly, 55*(4), 1167–1187.

Critchlow, J. (1988). Corruption Nationalism and the Native Elites in Soviet Central Asia. *The Journal of Communist Studies, 4*(2), 143–161.

Cummings, S. N. (2002). An uneasy relationship—Power and authority in the Nazarbayev regime. In S. N. Cummings (Ed.), *Power and change in Central Asia* (pp. 59–73). Routledge.
Cummings, S. N. (2005). *Kazakhstan power and elite*. I.B. Tauris.
Dahl, R. A. (Ed.). (1966). *Political oppositions in Western democracies*. Yale University Press.
Dahl, R. A. (1971). *Polyarchies: Participation and opposition*. Yale University Press.
Dahl, R. A. (1973). Introduction. In R. A. Dahl (Ed.), *Regimes and oppositions* (pp. 1–26). Yale University Press.
Dalmasso, E. (2018). Participation without representation: Moroccans abroad at a time of unstable authoritarian rule. *Globalizations, 15*(2), 198–214.
Darimbet, N. (2019, October 8). Ermurat Bali: novyi khozyin OSDP – beglyi oligarkh. *kz.media*. Accessed 26 Jan 2022. https://kz.media/archives/2499
Davenport, C. (2007). State repression and the tyrannical peace. *Journal of Peace Research, 44*(4), 485–504.
Dettman. (2018). *Dilemmas of opposition: Building parties and coalitions in authoritarian regimes*. Ph.D. dissertation. Cornell University.
Dimitrov, M. (2013). *Why communism did not collapse: Understanding authoritarian regime resilience in Asia and Europe*. Cambridge University Press.
Doszhanov, E. (2020, March 19). Mitingi i chrezvychaninye situatsii. Kakim byl pervyi god Tokayeva v Kazakhstane. *Nastoyashchee Vremya*. Accessed 14 Mar 2022. https://www.currenttime.tv/a/year-of-tokaev/30497260.html
Dowding, K., John, P., Mergoupis, T., & Van Vugt, M. (2000). Exit, voice and loyalty: Analytic and empirical developments. *European Journal of Political Research, 37*(4), 469–495.
Dubuisson, E. (2020). Whose world? Discourses of protection for land, environment, and natural resources in Kazakhstan. *Problems of Post-Communism*. https://doi.org/10.1080/10758216.2020.1788398
D'yachenko, S., Karmazina, L., and Seidumanov, S. (2000). *Politicheskie partii Kazakhstana god 2000 spravochnik*. Information-Analttical Centre of the Parliament of Kazakhstan.
Edgar, A. (2004). *Tribal nation: The making of Soviet Turkmenistan*. Princeton University Press.
Eurasian Centre of Political Research and the Agency for Social Technologies. (2005). *Gruppy vliyaniia vo vlastno-policheskoi sisteme Respubliki Kazakhstan*. Accessed 21 Dec. http://www.matritca.kz/news/34004-vspomnit-vse-gruppy-vliyaniya-vo-vlastno-politicheskoy-sisteme-respubliki-kazahstan-god-2005-y.html
Eurasian Transition Group. (2009). *The Aliev Dossier*. ETG.
Evans, A. (2012). Protests and civil society in Russia: The struggle for the Khimki forest. *Communist and Post-Communist Studies, 45*(3–4), 233–242.

Evans, G. (1998). Ethnic schism and the consolidation of post-communist democracies. *Communist and Post-Communist Studies, 31*(1), 57–74.

Ferghana.ru. (2016, April 27). V Kazakhstane idut nescanktsionirovannye mitingi protiv prodazhi zemli, nesmotrya na raz'yasnenie. *Ferghana.ru*. Accessed 25 Feb 2022. https://www.fergananews.com/news/24706

Forbes. (2019, July 17). Kto voshyol v Natsional'nyi sovet obshchestvennogo doveriya pri prezidente Kazakhstana. *Forbes*. Accessed 6 Mar 2022. https://forbes.kz/process/kto_voshel_v_natsionalnyiy_sovet_obschestvennogo_doveriya_pri_prezidente_kazahstana/

Frantz, E., & Kendall-Taylor, A. (2014). A dictator's toolkit: Understanding how co-optation affects repression in autocracies. *Journal of Peace Research, 51*(3), 332–346.

Friedrich, C., & Brzeinksi, Z. (1956). *Totalitarian dictatorship and autocracy*. Praeger.

Fuller, L. (1999, September 18). Kazakhstan's Kazhegeldin conspicuous by his absence. *Asia Times*. Accessed 29 Mar 2016. http://www.atimes.com/c-asia/AI18Ag02.html

Gainous, J., Wagner, K., & Ziegler, C. (2018). Digital media and political opposition in authoritarian systems: Russia's 2011 and 2016 Duma elections. *Democratization, 25*(2), 209–226.

Gandhi, J. (2008). *Political institutions under dictatorship*. Cambridge University. Press.

Gandhi, J., & Buckles, G. (2016, April 7–10). *Opposition unity and co-optation in hybrid regimes*. Paper Presented at the Annual Midwest Political Science Association Conference, Chicago, IL, pp. 1–33.

Gandhi, J., & Przeworski, A. (2006). Cooperation, co-optation, and rebellion under dictatorships. *Economics & Politics, 18*(1), 1–26.

Geddes, B. (2003). *Paradigms and sandcastles: Theory building and research design in comparative politics*. University of Michigan Press.

Geddes, B. (2006). *Why parties and elections in authoritarian regimes?* Presented at Annual Meeting of the American Political Science Association, Washington, DC.

Gel'man, V. (2005). Political opposition in Russia: A dying species? *Post-Soviet Affairs, 21*(3), 226–246.

Gel'man, V. (2015). Political opposition in Russia: A troubled transformation. *Europe-Asia Studies, 67*(2), 177–191.

Giddens, A. (1994). *The constitution of society introduction of the theory of structuration*. University of California Press.

Glasius, M. (2018). What authoritarianism is ... and is not: A practice perspective. *International Affairs, 94*(3), 515–533.

Gleason, G. (1991). Fealty and loyalty: Informal authority structures in Soviet Asia. *Soviet Studies, 43*(4), 613–628.

Gleason, G. (1997). *The Central Asian states: Discovering independence*. Westview Press.
Global Witness. (2012). *Risky business: Kazakhstan, Kazakhmys PLC and the London Stock Exchange*. Global Witness.
Glushkova, S. (2011, August 8). Aktivist neftyanikov Natalya Sokolova osyzhdena na shest' let tyur'my. *Radio Azattyk*. Accessed online 24 Jan 2022. https://rus.azattyq.org/a/natalya_sokolova_oil_workers_lawyer_verdict/24290171.html
Gorlizki, Y., & Khlevniuk, O. (2020). *Substate dictatorship: Networks, loyalty, and institutional change in the Soviet Union*. Yale University Press.
Gorst, I. (2013, July 5). Mukhtar Ablyazov at centre of fight over Kazakhstan's BTA Bank. *Financial Times*. Accessed 31 Mar 2016. http://www.ft.com/cms/s/0/23571482-e584-11e2-ad1a-00144feabdc0.html#axzz3wCYbKtZ7
Grosin, A. (2005). *Kto est kto v sovremenom Kazakhstane. Zanimatel'no – o klanovykh gruppirovkakh*. Instituta Stran SNG.
Hahn, G. (1994). Opposition politics in Russia. *Europe-Asia Studies, 46*(2), 305–355.
Hale, H. (2014). *Patronal politics: Eurasian regime dynamics in comparative perspective*. Cambridge University Press.
Harvey, C. (2011). Changes in the menu of manipulation: Electoral fraud, ballot stuffing, and voter pressure in the 2011 Russian election. *Electoral Studies, 41*(3), 105–117.
Haugbølle, R. H., & Cavatorta, F. (2011). Will the real Tunisian opposition please stand up? Opposition coordination failures under authoritarian constraints. *British Journal of Middle Eastern Studies, 38*(3), 323–341.
Haugen, A. (2003). *The establishment of national republics in Soviet Central Asia*. Palgrave Macmillan.
Heibach, J., & Transfeld, M. (2018). Opposition dynamism under authoritarianism: The case of Yemen, 1994–2011. *Democratization, 25*(4), 597–613.
Helms, L. (2004). Five ways of institutionalizing political opposition: Lessons from the advanced democracies. *Government and Opposition, 39*(1), 22–54.
Helms, L. (2021). Introduction: The nature of political opposition in contemporary electoral democracies and autocracies. *European Political Science, 20*(April), 569–579.
Hencken Ritter, E., & Conrad, C. R. (2016). Preventing and responding to dissent: The observational challenges of explaining strategic repression. *American Political Science Review, 110*(1), 85–99.
Hensby, A. (2017). Open networks and secret Facebook groups: Exploring cycle effects on activists' social media use in the 2010/11 UK student protests. *Social Movement Studies, 16*(4), 466–478.
Hirschman, A. (1970). *Exit, voice and loyalty: Responses to decline in firms, organizations and states*. Harvard University Press.

Hirschman, A. (1993). Exit, voice, and the fate of the German democratic republic: An essay in conceptual history. *World Politics, 45*(2), 173–202.

Hoffmann, B. (2010). Bringing Hirschman back in: "Exit", "voice" and "loyalty" in the politics of transnational migration. *The Latin Americanist, 54*(2), 57–73.

Hooghe, M., Marien, S., & Pauwels, T. (2011). Where do distrusting voters turn if there is no viable exit or voice option? The impact of political trust on electoral behaviour in the Belgian regional elections of June 2009. *Government and Opposition, 46*(2), 245–273.

Hough, J. (1983). Pluralism, corporatism and the Soviet Union. In S. G. Solomon (Ed.), *Pluralism in the Soviet Union essays in honour of H. Gordon Skilling* (pp. 37–60). Macmillan Press.

Human Rights Watch. (2012a, June 4). Kazakhstan: Oil workers convicted in flawed trial. *Human Rights Watch*. Accessed online 6 Mar 2022. https://www.hrw.org/news/2012/06/04/kazakhstan-oil-workers-convicted-flawed-trial

Human Rights Watch. (2012b, October 9). Kazakhstan: Opposition leader jailed. *Human Rights Watch*. Accessed 6 Mar 2012. https://www.hrw.org/news/2012/10/09/kazakhstan-opposition-leader-jailed

Ilkhamov, A. (2007). Neopatrimonialism, interest groups and patronage networks: The impasses of the governance system in Uzbekistan. *Central Asian Survey, 26*(1), 65–84.

Inosmi. (2016, May 6). Zemel'nye protesty otrazhenie nedovol'stva obshchim polozheniem del v strane? *Inosmi*. Accessed 25 Feb. https://inosmi.ru/20160506/236436458.html

Ionescu, G., & de Madariaga, I. (1968). *Opposition: Past and present of a political institution*. C. A. Watts and Co. Ltd.

Ionescu, G., & de Madariaga, I. (1972). *Opposition: Past and present of a political institution*. Penguin Books, Ltd.

Isaacs, R. (2008). Managing dissent limiting risk and consolidating power: The processes and results of constitutional reform in Kazakhstan. *Central Asia and the Caucasus, 44*(1), 16–25.

Isaacs, R. (2011). *Party system formation in Kazakhstan: Between formal and informal politics*. Routledge.

Isaacs, R. (2014). Neopatrimonialism and beyond! Re-assessing the formal and informal in Central Asian politics. *Contemporary Politics, 20*(2), 229–245.

Isaacs, R. (2018). *Film and identity in Kazakhstan: Soviet and post-Soviet culture*. I.B. Tauris.

Isaacs, R., & Polese, A. (2015). Between "imagined" and "real" nation-building: Identities and nationhood in post-Soviet Central Asia. *Nationalities Papers, 43*(3), 371–382.

Isaacs, R., & Whitmore, S. (2014). The limited agency and life-cycles of personalized dominant parties in the post-Soviet space: The cases of United Russia and Nur Otan. *Democratization, 21*(4) 699–721.

Ishiyama, J. (2002). Neopatrimonialism and the prospects for democratization in the Central Asian Republics. In S. N. Cummings (Ed.), *Power and change in Central Asia* (pp. 42–58). Routledge.

IWRP. (2022, February 11). Nazarbayev's fading personality cult. *Institute for War and Peace Reporting*. Accessed 6 Mar 2022. https://iwpr.net/global-voi ces/kazakstan-nazarbayevs-fading-personality-cult

Jardine, B., Khashimov, S., Lemon, E., & Kyzy, A. (2021). *Mapping patterns of dissent in Eurasia: Introducing the Central Asia protest tracker*. Oxus Society for Central Asian Affairs.

Junisbai, B. (2010). A tale of two Kazakhstans: Sources of political cleavage and conflict in the post-soviet period. *Europe-Asia Studies, 62*(2), 235–269.

Junisbai, B., & Junisbai, A. (2005). The democratic choice of Kazakhstan: A case study in economic liberalization, intra-elite cleavage and political opposition. *Demokratizatsiya: The Journal of Post-Soviet Democratization, 13*(2), 373–392.

Kazhegeldin, A. (1998a). *Kazakhstan: pravo vybora*. Karzhy Karzhat.

Kazhegeldin, A. (1998b). *Akezhan Kazhegeldin announces candidacy for the presidency of Kazakhstan*. Accessed 29 Mar 2016. http://www.prnewswire. com/news-releases/akezhan-kazhegeldin-announces-candidacy-for-the-presid ency-of-kazakhstan-76947707.html

Kazinform. (2004, October 19). Zharmakhan Tuyakbai zayavil o vykhode is partii Otan. *Nomad*. Accessed 25 Mar 2016. http://www.nomad.su/?a=3-200410 190019

Kennedy, R. (2006). A Colorless election: The 2005 presidential election in Kazakhstan, and what it means for the future of the opposition. *Problems of Post Communism, 53*(6), 46–58.

Kesici, O. (2017). The Alash movement and the question of Kazakh ethnicity. *Nationalities Papers, 45*(6), 1135–1149.

Kevlihan, R., & Ó Beacháin, D. (2017). Menus of manipulation: Authoritarian continuities in Central Asian elections. *Demokratizatsiya: The Journal of Post-Soviet Democratization, 25*(4), 407–434.

Khamidov, A. (2011, August 22). Kazakhstan: Labor unrest denting Astana's economic image. *Eurasianet*. Accessed 24 Jan 2022. http://www.eurasianet. org/node/64077. Accessed 9 Sept 2014.

Khulupin, V. N. (2000, April 22). *Kazakhstanskaia Politicheskaia elita mezhdu modernizatsiei i traibalizom*. Report to the Second All-Russian Congress of Political Scientists, Moscow MGIMO. Accessed 21 Dec 2021. https://www. neweurasia.info/archive/2000/top5/05_26_26.051.htm

Kitschelt, H., Mansfeldova, Z., Markowski, R., & Tóka, G. (1999). *Post-communist party systems: Competition, representation, and inter-party cooperation*. Cambridge University Press.

Koch, N. (2018). Disorder over the border: Spinning the spectre of instability through time and space in Central Asia. *Central Asian Survey, 37*(1), 13–30.

Koesel, K., & Bunce, V. (2012). Putin, popular protests, and political trajectories in Russia: A comparative perspective. *Post-Soviet Affairs, 28*(4), 403–423.

Koigeldiev, M. (2007). The Alash movement and the Soviet government: A difference of positions. In U. Tomohiko (Ed.), *Empire, Islam, and politics in Central Eurasia*. Slavic Research Centre, Hokkaido University.

Kostyuchenko, E. (2011, December 20). Zhanaozen. *Novaya Gazeta*. Accessed 25 Jan 2022. https://novayagazeta.ru/articles/2011/12/20/47465-zhanaozen

Kudaibergenova, D. T. (2019). Compartmentalized ideology: Presidential addresses and Legitimation in Kazakhstan. In R. Isaacs & A. Frigerio (Eds.), *Theorizing Central Asian politics: The state, ideology and power* (pp. 145–166). Palgrave Macmillan.

Kumenov, A. (2021, February 23). Kazakhstan: Workers increasingly resorting to strikes, and succeeding. *Eurasianet*. Accessed 18 Jan 2022. https://eurasianet.org/kazakhstan-workers-increasingly-resorting-to-strikes-and-succeeding

Kumenov, A. (2022, January 17). Key Nazarbayev cronies undergo apparent purge. *Eurasianet*. Accessed 6 Mar 2022. https://eurasianet.org/kazakhstan-key-nazarbayev-cronies-undergo-apparent-purge

Kusainov, A. (2005, November 13). Mysterious murder mars presidential election campaign. *Eurasianet*. Accessed 2 Apr 2016. http://www.eurasianet.org/departments/insight/articles/eav111405.shtml

Lakhanuly, N. (2015, April 18). Intelligentsiya prizyvaet Nazarbayeva byt' ostorozhnym. *Radio Azattyk*. Accessed 20 Feb 2022. https://rus.azattyq.org/a/zemelniy-vopros-obraschenie-k-nazarbaevu/27680758.html

Landgrave, M., & Nowrasteh, A. (2016). Voice, exit, and liberty: The effect of emigration on origin country institutions. *Economic Development Bulletin, 25*, 1–4.

Langston, J. (2002). Breaking out is hard to do: Exit, voice, and loyalty in Mexico's one-party hegemonic regime. *Latin American Politics and Society, 44*(3), 61–88.

La Porte, J. (2014). Hidden in plain sight: Political opposition and hegemonic authoritarianism in Azerbaijan. *Post-Soviet Affairs, 31*(4), 339–366.

La Porte, J. (2017) Foreign versus Domestic Bribery: Explaining Repression in Kleptocratic Regimes. *Comparative Politics, 50*(1), 83–102.

Laruelle, M. (2019). 'The Nazarbayev generation: A sociological portrait', lives'. In M. Laruelle (Ed.), *The Nazarbayev generation: Youth in Kazakhstan* (pp. 1–24). Rowman & Littlefield.

Laštro, C., & Bieber, F. (2021). The performance of opposition parties in competitive authoritarian regimes: Three case studies from the Western Balkans. *European Political Science, 20*(March), 617–629.

Lewis, D. (2016). Blogging Zhanaozen: Hegemonic discourse and authoritarian resilience in Kazakhstan. *Central Asian Survey, 35*(3), 421–438.

Liber, G. (1991). Korenizatsiia: Restructuring Soviet nationality policy in the 1920s. *Ethnic and Racial Studies, 14*(1), 15–23.

Lieven, A. (1993). *The Baltic revolution: Estonia, Latvia, Lithuania and the path to independence*. Yale University Press.

Lillis, J. (2007, June 12). The domestic implications of Rakhat Aliev's precipitous fall. *Eurasianet*. Accessed 13 June 2007. http://www.eurasianet.org/departments/insight/articles/eav061307f.shtml

Lillis, J. (2011a, October 13). Kazakhstan: Labor dispute dragging energy production down. *Eurasianet*. Accessed 24 Jan 2022. https://eurasianet.org/kazakhstan-labor-dispute-dragging-energy-production-down

Lillis, J. (2011b, September 6). Kazakhstan: Astana confronts extremist threat. *Eurasianet*. Accessed 20 Jan 2022. https://eurasianet.org/kazakhstan-astana-confronts-extremist-threat

Lillis, J. (2012a, October 10). Kazakhstan: Political trial fails to provoke Pussy Riot-Style outcry. *Eurasianet*. Accessed 31 Mar 2016. http://www.eurasianet.org/node/66330

Lillis, J. (2012b, December 21). Kazakhstan: Court shuts key opposition party. *Eurasianet*. Accessed 31 Mar 2016. http://www.eurasianet.org/node/66032

Lillis, J. (2012c, April 23). Kazakhstan: Rights activists urge halt to Zhanaozen trial amid torture claims. *Eurasianet*. Accessed 30 Jan 2022. http://www.eurasianet.org/node/66032

Lillis, J. (2016a, May 24). Kazakhstan: Land issue fuelling social discontent. *Eurasianet*. Accessed 25 May 2016. https://eurasianet.org/kazakhstan-land-issue-fueling-social-discontent

Lillis, J. (2016b, June 1). Kazakhstan: Mud-slinging at protesters highlights apparent media double standards. *Eurasianet*. Accessed 3 June 2016. https://eurasianet.org/kazakhstan-mud-slinging-protesters-highlights-apparent-media-double-standards

Lillis, J. (2016c, June 6). Kazakhstan: Businessman accused of stoking land protests as coup plot. *Eurasianet*. Accessed 9 June 2016. https://eurasianet.org/kazakhstan-businessman-accused-stoking-land-protests-coup-plot

Lillis, J. (2019, January 21). Kazakhstan: The mothers that became the faces of dissent. *Eurasianet*. Accessed 31 Jan 2022. https://eurasianet.org/kazakhstan-the-mothers-that-became-the-faces-of-dissent

Lillis, J. (2022, January 7). Shoot to kill protesters, orders tough-talking Tokayev. *Eurasianet*. Accessed 5 Mar 2022. https://eurasianet.org/kazakhstan-shoot-to-kill-protesters-orders-tough-talking-tokayev

Linz, J. J. (1973). Opposition in and under Authoritarian regime: The case of Spain. In R. Dahl (Ed.), *Regimes and oppositions* (pp. 171–259). Yale University Press.

Linz, J. J. (2000). *Totalitarian and authoritarian regimes*. Lynne Rienner.

Loginova, O. (2022, January 10). Yevgenii Zhovtis, pravozashchitnik 'posle etikh sobytii budet soblazn v kakoi-to stepeni zakrychivat'. *Vlast.kz*. Accessed 5 Mar 2022. https://vlast.kz/politika/48096-evgenij-zovtis-pravozasitnik-posle-etih-sobytij-budet-soblazn-v-kakoj-to-stepeni-zakrucivat-gajki.html

Lust-Okar, E. (2005). *Structuring conflict in the Arab world: Incumbents, opponents, and institutions*. Cambridge University Press.

Magaloni, B. (2008). Credible power-sharing and the longevity of authoritarian rule. *Comparative Political Studies, 41*(4/5), 715–741.

Magaloni, B., & Kricheli, R. (2010). Political order and one-party rule. *The Annual Review of Political Science, 13*, 123–143.

Maher, T., & Peterson, L. (2008). Time and country variation in contentious politics: Multilevel modelling of dissent and repression. *International Journal of Sociology, 38*(3), 52–81.

Makhmutova, M., & Akhmetova, A. (2011). *Civil Society Index in Kazakhstan: CIVICUS Civil Society Index 2008–2010: Analytical country report*. Civicus.

Malesky, E., & Schuler, P. (2010). Nodding or needling: Analyzing delegate responsiveness in an authoritarian parliament. *American Political Science Review, 104*(3), 482–502.

Mamashuly, A. (2020, January 28). Konstitutsiya kotoraya ne ustroila Nazarbayeva. Osnovnoi zakon 1993 goda. *Radio Azattyk*. Accessed 19 Dec 2021. https://rus.azattyq.org/a/kazakhstan-constitution-1993-parliament-and-presidential-powers/30401326.html

Marat, E. (2016). Post-violence regime survival and expansion in Kazakhstan and Tajikistan. *Central Asian Survey, 35*(4), 531–548.

March, L. (2009). Managing opposition in a hybrid regime: Just Russia and parastatal opposition. *Slavic Review, 68*(3), 504–527.

Markham, T. (2014). Social media, protest cultures and political subjectivities of the Arab Spring. *Media, Culture & Society, 36*(1), 89–104.

Masanov, N. (2000). Political elite in Kazakhstan: The changes of Kazakhstani political elite during the period of sovereignty. *International Eurasian Institute for Economic and Political Research*. Almaty. Accessed 16 Apr 2009. http://iicas.org/english/publ_22_11_00.htm

Mazorenko, D., & Kaisar, A. (2022, January 27). On the ground in Kazakhstan's protests: What really happened? *Open Democracy*. Accessed 5 Mar 2022. https://www.opendemocracy.net/en/odr/what-really-happened-kazakhstan-protests-january/

Michaelsen, M. (2018). Exit and voice in a digital age: Iran's exiled activists and the authoritarian state. *Globalizations, 15*(2), 248–264.

Moore, M. (1998). Repression and dissent: Substitution, context, and timing. *American Journal of Political Science, 42*(3), 851–873.
Moore, M. (2000). The repression of dissent: A substitution model of government coercion. *The Journal of Conflict Resolution, 44*(1), 107–127.
Moses, W. (2005). Exit, vote and sovereignty: Migration, sates and globalization. *Review of International Political Economy, 12*(1), 53–77.
Muminov, A. (2013). Oppozitsiya v Kazakhstane. Klient, ckoree, mertv, Kursiv, 20 September. Accessed 4 December 2013. http://www.kursiv.kz/news/obshestvo/Oppozitciya-v-Kazahstane-Klientskoree-mertv/
Mukankyzy, M. (2014, April 6). Dekabr'skie sobytiya v uchebnikakh istorii. *Radio Azattyk*. Accessed 17 Dec 2021. https://rus.azattyq.org/a/kazakhstan-december-events-in-schoolbooks/25221330.html
Mukhanov, B. (2018, March 13). Partiyu Ablayzova DVK priznali ekstremistskoi organizatsiei v Kazakhstane. *InformBuro*. Accessed 19 Jan 2022. https://informburo.kz/novosti/partiyu-ablyazova-dvk-priznali-ekstremistkoy-organizaciey-v-kazahstane-.html
Muminov, A. (2015, April 24). Vechnoe vozvrashchenie – Akezhana Kazhegeldina prizovut v preddverii cereznykh reform? *Kursiv*. Accessed 16 May 2015. http://www.kursiv.kz/news/vlast/vechnoe_vozvrashchenie_akezhana_kazhegeldina_prizovut_v_preddverii_sereznykh_reform_916/
Najibullah, F. (2019, February 12). Tragic fire in Astana gives Kazakh mothers' protests new momentum. *Radio Free Europe/Radio Liberty*. Accessed 19 Jan 2022. https://www.rferl.org/a/tragic-fire-in-astana-gives-kazakh-mothers-protests-new-momentum/29765930.html
Najibullah, F. (2022, March 18). Kazakh president unlikely to give up real power despite pledging end to 'super-presidency'. *Radio Free Europe/Radio Liberty*. Accessed 18 Mar 2022. https://www.rferl.org/a/kazakhstan-toqaev-reforms-analysis/31759365.html
Nasimova, G. O., Buzurtanova, M. M., & Saitova, N. A. (2019). Social protests in Kazakhstan: Factors and trends. *Philosophy and Conflict Studies, 35*(3), 472–484.
Nazarbayev, N. (1992). *Without right and left*. Class Publishing.
Noble, B. (2020). Authoritarian amendments: Legislative institutions as intraexecutive constraints in post-Soviet Russia. *Comparative Political Studies, 53*(9), 1417–1454.
Nomad. (2004, May 12). V Kazakhstane likvidrovany chetyre parti. *nomad*. Accessed 12 Oct 2008. http://www.nomad.su/?a=3-200405120021
Norton, P. (2008). Making sense of opposition. *The Journal of Legislative Studies, 14*(1–2), 236–250.
O'Donnell, G. (1986). On the fruitful convergences of Hirschman's exit, voice, and loyalty and shifting involvements: Reflections from the recent Argentine experience. In A. Foxley, M. S. McPherson, G. A. O'Donnell, and A. O.

Hirschman (Eds.), *Development, democracy, and the art of trespassing: Essays in honour of Albert O. Hirschman* (pp. 251–252). University of Notre Dame Press.

O'Donnell, G. (1988). *Bureaucratic authoritarianism: Argentina, 1966–1973 in comparative perspective*. University of California Press.

O'Donnell, G., & Schmitter, P. (1986). *Transitions from authoritarian rule: Tentative conclusions about uncertain democracies* (Vol. 4). John Hopkins University Press.

Olcott, M. (1987). *The Kazakhs*. Hoover Institution Press.

Olcott, M. (1997). Nursultan Nazarbayev as a strong president. In R. Taras (Ed.), *Post-communist presidents*. Cambridge University Press.

Olcott, M. (2002). *Kazakhstan unfulfilled promise*. Brookings Institution Press.

Orazgaliyeva, M. (2016, June 9). Kazakh president declares June 9 as national day of mourning. *Astana Times*. Accessed 20 Jan 2022. https://astanatimes.com/2016/06/kazakh-president-declares-june-9-as-national-day-of-mourning/

OSCE/ODHIR. (2004). *Republic of Kazakhstan parliamentary elections 19 September and 3 October 2004: OSCE/ODIHR election observation mission report*. OSCE/ODIHR.

Pannier, B. (2020, January 20). Kazakh officials force protesters into faraway places for opposition rallies. *Radio Free Europe/Radio Liberty*. Accessed 18 Jan 2022. https://www.rferl.org/a/kazakh-officials-force-protesters-into-faraway-places-for-opposition-rallies/30387955.html

Paterson. (2015, March 15). Rakhat Aliyev: Claims of murder over death of rival to Kazakhstan's president in Austrian prison. *The Independent*. Accessed 31 Mar 2016. http://www.independent.co.uk/news/world/asia/rakhat-aliyev-claims-of-murder-over-death-of-rival-to-kazakhstans-president-in-an-austrian-prison-10108693.html

Pearce, K. (2014). Two can play at that game: Social media opportunities in Azerbaijan for government and opposition. *Demokratizatsiya, 22*(1), 39–66.

Pearce, K., & Hajizada, A. (2014). No laughing matter humor as a means of dissent in the digital era: The case of authoritarian Azerbaijan. *Demokratizatsiya, 22*(1), 67–85.

Pepinsky, T. (2014). The institutional turn in comparative authoritarianism. *British Journal of Political Science, 44*(3), 631–653.

Peyrouse, S. (2012). The Kazakh Neopatrimonial regime: Balancing uncertainties among the "family," oligarchs and technocrats. *Demokratizatsiya, 20*(4), 345–370.

Pfaff, S., & Kim, H. (2003). Exit-voice dynamics in collective action: An analysis of emigration and protest in the East German revolution. *American Journal of Sociology, 109*(2), 401–444.

Pirani, S. (2021, December 21). Who fired the shots? *The Ecologist.* Accessed online 24 January 2022. https://theecologist.org/2021/dec/16/who-fired-shots

Pomfret, R. (2005). Kazakhstan's economy since independence: Does the oil boom offer a second chance for sustainable development? *Europe-Asia Studies, 57*(6), 859–876.

Ponomarev, V. A. (1991). *Obshchestvennye organizatsii v Kazakhstane i Kyrgyzstane (1987–1991).* Glagol.

Press Service of RNPK. (2001, September 7). Zaochnyi sud nad Kazhegeldinym kak rezul'tat politiki bezzakoniia i proizvola. *Press Service of RNPK.* Accessed 26 June 2008. http://kazhegeldin.addr.com/articles/About_07_09_01_3.htm

Procuror.kz. (2004, December 13). Zayavlenie o likvidatsii yridicheskogo litsa. *Procuror.kz.* Accessed 3 May 2007. http://www.procuror.kz/?iid=5&type=news&lang=ru&nid=61

Pron, E., & Szwajnoch, E. (2019, October 31). Kazakh anti-Chinese protests and the issue of Xinjiang detention camps. *The Central Asia-Caucasus Analyst.* Accessed 18 Jan 2022. http://www.cacianalyst.org/publications/analytical-articles/item/13593-kazakh-anti-chinese-protests-and-the-issue-of-xinjiang-detention-camps.html

Radio Azattyk. (2016a, May 21). 21 Maya 2016 goda zaderzhaniya i blokirovki. *Radio Azattyk.* Accessed 23 May 2016. http://rus.azattyq.org/a/kazakhstan-mitingi-protesta-zemelnaya-reforma-azattyq/27748653.html

Radio Azattyk. (2016b, November 28). Bokaeva i Ayna prigovorili k tyuremnym srokam. *Radio Azattyk.* Accessed 25 Feb 2022. https://rus.azattyq.org/a/atyrau-ayan-bokaev-prigovor/28143089.html

Radio Azattyk. (2019a, May 1). "Boikot i Narod ustal!" Nesanktsionirovannye aktsii I zaderzhaniya v Nur-Suttane i Almaty. *Radio Azattyk.* Accessed 7 June 2020. https://rus.azattyq.org/a/kazakhstan-nur-sultan-almaty-rally-1-may/29914075.html

Radio Azattyk. (2019b, May 2). Protesty 1 Maya. Ka keto bylo. *Radio Azattyk.* Accessed 3 Mar 2022. https://rus.azattyq.org/a/kazakhstan-1-may-protest/29915649.html

Radio Azattyk. (2019c, June 21). Dvuzhenie Oyan Kazakhstan provelo aktsiyu seruen v gorodakh Kazakhstana. *Radio Azattyk.* Accessed 7 June 2020. https://rus.azattyq.org/a/30012986.html

Radio Azattyk. (2019d, June 9). Massovye zaderzhaniya i soobshcheniya o narushcheniya v den' golosovaniya. *Radio Azattyk.* Accessed 6 Mar. https://rus.azattyq.org/a/kazakhstan-detentions-presidential-election-9-june/29989331.html

Radio Azattyk. (2019e, May 9). Den' pobedy nad zdravym smyslom. Blokirovki i zaderzhaniya 9 May. *Radio Azattyk*. Accessed 9 May 2019. https://rus.aza ttyq.org/a/kazakhstan-9-maya-blokirovki-zaderzhania/29930113.html

Radio Azattyk. (2020, November 27). OSDP pb'yavila boikot vyboram Ablyazov schitate, chto partyiya vypolnyaet 'prikaz'. *Radio Azattyk*. Accessed 26 Jan. https://rus.azattyq.org/a/kazakhstan-party-to-boycott-january-parlia mentary-elections/30971975.html

Radio Azattyk. (2022, January 5). Kak snosili pamyatnik. *Radio Azattyk*. Accessed 6 Mar 2022. https://rus.azattyq.org/a/31641005.html

Radionov, V. (2020, December 25). Clyshayut, no ne slyshat. Yevgenii Zhovtis o glukhom gosudarstve. *Kz.media*. Accessed 5 Mar 2022. https://kz.media/archives/36985

Regnum. (2016, May 5). Nazarbaev otstupil: chinovniki budut cledit' za nastroeniyami v sotsetyakh. *Regnum*. Accessed 28 Dec 2018. https://reg num.ru/news/polit/2128839.html

Reuter, J. O., & Robertson, G. (2015). Legislatures, cooptation, and social protest in contemporary authoritarian regimes. *The Journal of Politics, 77*(1), 235–248.

Rittmann, M. (2020, May 28). Kazakhstan's 'reformed' protest law hardly an improvement. *Human Rights Watch*. Accessed 22 Jan 2022. https://www.hrw.org/news/2020/05/28/kazakhstans-reformed-pro test-law-hardly-improvement

Rittmann, M. (2021, July 22). A sustained crackdown on independent worker organising—Kazakhstan, a case study. *The Foreign Policy Centre*. Accessed 30 Jan 2022. https://fpc.org.uk/a-sustained-crackdown-on-independent-wor ker-organising-kazakhstan-a-case-study/

Ross, M. H. (1988). Political organization and political participation: Exit, voice and loyalty in pre-industrial societies. *Comparative Politics, 21*(1), 73–89.

Roy, O. (2000). *The New Central Asia: The creation of nations*. I.B. Tauris.

Rustow, D. (1970). Transitions to democracy: Toward a dynamic model. *Comparative Politics, 2*(3), 337–363.

Sabol, S. (1995). The creation of Soviet Central Asia: The 1924 national delimitation. *Central Asian Survey, 14*(2), 225–241.

Salmon, P. (2011). Repression intensifies against Kazakh oil workers' uprising. *Debatte: Journal of Contemporary Central and Eastern Europe, 19*(1–2), 507–510.

Salmon, P. (2012). Police Massacre has opened a dark chapter for Kazakh workers' movement. *Debatte: Journal of Contemporary Central and Eastern Europe, 20*(1), 73–77.

Sanghera, B., & Satybaldieva, E. (2021). *Rentier capitalism and its discontents: Power, morality and resistance in Central Asia*. Palgrave Macmillan.

Sansei, D. (2019, May 2). Chto stalo s zaderzhannymi i kto oni. *Radio Azattyk*. Accessed 6 Mar 2022. https://rus.azattyq.org/a/kazakhstan-what-happened-to-people-during-a-rally-on-may-1st/29917561.html

Sartori, G. (1966). Opposition and control problems and prospects. *Government and Opposition, 1*(1), 149–154.

Satpayev, D. (2015, February 24). Rakhat Aliev ne predstavlyal ugrozy vlastyam Kazakhstana. *Kursiv*. Accessed 27 Feb 2015. http://www.kursiv.kz/news/vlast/rakhat_aliev_ne_predstavlyal_ugrozy_vlastyam_kazakhstana_d_satpaev_166/

Satpayev, D., & Umbetaliyeva, T. (2015). The protests in Zhanaozen and the Kazakh oil sector: Conflicting interests in a Rentier State. *Journal of Eurasian Studies, 6*(2), 122–129.

Schapiro, L. (1967). Putting the lid on Leninism: Opposition and dissent in the communist one-party states. *Government and Opposition, 2*(2), 181–203.

Schatz, E. (2009). The soft authoritarian tool kit: Agenda-setting power in Kazakhstan and Kyrgyzstan. *Comparative Politics, 41*(2), 203–222.

Schedler, A. (2002). The menu of manipulation. *Journal of Democracy, 13*(2), 36–50.

Schedler, A. (2006). *Electoral authoritarianism: The dynamics of unfree competition*. Lynne Rienner.

Schmitter, P. (1974). Still the century of corporatism? *The Review of Politics, 36*(1), 85–131.

Sdykov, M. (2012). *Istoriiya Zapadnogo otdelniya Alash-Ordy*. Zapadno-Kazakhstanskii oblastnoi tsentr istorii i arkheologii.

Selçuk, O., & Hekimci, D. (2020). The rise of the democracy—Authoritarianism cleavage and opposition coordination in Turkey (2014–2019). *Democratization, 27*(8), 1496–1514.

Semenov, A. (2017). Against the stream: Political opposition in the Russian regions during the 2012–2016 electoral cycle. *Demokratizatsiya, 25*(4), 481–502.

Shkel, S., & Shakirova, E. V. (2014). Political opposition in the hybrid regime: Post-Soviet Russia experience. *Review of Political Science, 1*, 4–21.

Sholk, D. (2016, June 15). Kazakhstan's land reforms. *The Diplomat*. Accessed 20 June 2016. https://thediplomat.com/2016/06/kazakhstans-land-reforms/

Shurga, S. (1999, September 25). Delo Kazhegel'dina prodolzhaetsya. *Nezavisimaya Gazeta*. Accessed online 7 Jan 2022. https://www.ng.ru/cis/1999-09-25/kazhegeldin.html

Silitski, V. (2005). Preempting democracy: The case of Belarus. *Journal of Democracy, 16*(4), 83–97.

Sindelar, D. (2013, March 31). How far will Nazarbaev go to take down Mukhtar Ablyazov? *RFE/RL*. Accessed 2 Apr 2013. http://www.rferl.org/content/kazakhstan-nazarbaev-ablyazov/25010488.html

Sippola, M. (2013). The awkward choices facing the baltic worker: Exit or loyalty. *Journal of Baltic Studies, 44*(4), 451–473.

Smaiyl, M. (2019, September 2). Tokaev o mitingakh: Nuzhno razreshat' i vydelyat' mesta ne na okraonakh. *Tengrinews*. Accessed 5 Mar 2022. https://tengrinews.kz/kazakhstan_news/tokaev-mitingah-nujno-razreshat-vyidelyat-mesta-na-okrainah-378015/

Socialism.kz.info. (2011, May 30). Press-reliz aktivistov profsoyuza 'Karazhanbasmunai' po fakty aresta Natal'i Sokolovoi i presledovaniya bastyushchikh neftyanikov. *Socialism.kz.info*. Accessed 12 Feb 2022. http://socialismkz.info/?p=2206

Stepan, A. (1997). Democratic opposition and democratization theory. *Government and Opposition, 32*(4), 657–663.

Sultanova, S. (2014). Challenging the Aliyev regime: Political opposition in Azerbaijan. *Demokratizatsiya, 22*(1), 15–37.

Svolik, M. (2012). *The politics of authoritarian rule*. Cambridge University Press.

Taukina, R. (2005, April 29). Raskol v partii AK Zhol: Konflikt liderov ili idei? *Club Polyton*. Accessed 6 Oct 2006. http://www.club.kz/index.php?lang=en&mod=analitics&submod=self&article=310

The Village. (2019, March 25). Eto imya dal mne dedushka v chest' sami znaete kogo: Nursultan yob imeni Astane i president. *The Village*. Accessed 6 June 2020. https://www.the-village.kz/village/people/people/5229-menya-zovut-nursultan

Toguzbaev, K. (2011a, July 7). Kolbina pokazali kazakhskim rukovoditelyam eshche letom 1986 goda. *Radio Azattyk*. Accessed 17 Dec 2021. https://rus.azattyq.org/a/zakash_kamalidenov_1986_book_/24255023.html

Toguzbaev, K. (2011b, December 22). Nazarbayev v Zhanaozene. *Radio Azattyk*. Accessed 30 Jan 2022. https://rus.azattyq.org/a/nursultan_nazarbaev_unrest_in_mangistau_province/24430106.html

Toguzbaev, K. (2018, June 13). Shanyrak 12 let spustya. Sobytiya, o kotorykh zabyvayut? *Radio Azattyk*. Accessed 18 Jan 2022. https://rus.azattyq.org/a/shanyrakskiye-sobytia-12-let-spustya/29356950.html

Toiken, S. (2016, April 14). Protest v Atyray protiv prodazhi zemli. *Radio Azattyk*. Accessed 24 Feb 2022. https://rus.azattyq.org/a/protest-v-atyrau-protiv-prodazhi-zemel-inostrantsam/27693602.html

Toleukhanova, A. (2016a, September 20). Kazakhstan: Mortgage rallies continue despite protest fears. *Eurasianet*. Accessed online 18 Jan 2022. https://eurasianet.org/kazakhstan-mortgage-rallies-continue-despite-protest-fears

Toleukhanova, A. (2016b, July 18). Kazakhstan's latest shooting: Terror or crime? *Eurasianet*. Accessed 20 Jan 2022. https://eurasianet.org/kazakh stans-latest-shooting-terror-or-crime

Toleukhanova, A. (2016c, May 6). Zemel'ne protesty – otrazhenie nedovol'stva obshchim polozheniem del v strane? *Eurasianet*. Accessed 20 Feb 2022. https://inosmi.ru/20160506/236436458.html

Totaro, M., & Sorbello, P. (2021). Oil, capital and labour around the caspian. In R. Isaacs & E. Marat (Eds.), *The Routledge handbook of contemporary Central Asia*. Routledge.

Trotsenko, P. (2017, January 23). Neudobnaya profsoyuznaya organizatsiya. *Radio Azattyk*. Accessed 30 Jan 2022. https://rus.azattyq.org/a/neudob naya-profsouznaya-organyzacia/28251081.html

Turebekova, A. (2016, August 23). Kazakhstan extends by five years moratorium on controversial land code amendments. *The Astana Times*. Accessed 28 Dec 2016. https://astanatimes.com/2016/08/kazakhstan-extends-by-five-years-moratorium-on-controversial-land-code-amendments/

Turgaev, S. (2022, January 6). Ya porazhayus' terpeniyu etogo naroda. Byvshii prem'er Kazakhstana – o prichinakh massovykh protestov v strane. *Nastoyashchee Vremya*. Accessed 11 Jan 2022. https://www.currenttime.tv/a/byv shiy-premyer-kazakhstana/31642149.html

Turovsky, R. (2014). Opposition parties in hybrid regimes: Between repression and co-optation: The case of Russia's regions. *Perspectives on European Politics and Society, 15*(1), 68–87.

Ubiria, G. (2016). *Soviet nation-building in Central Asia: The making of the Kazakh and Uzbek Nations*. Routledge.

Vaal, T. (2022, January 27). S Nazarbayevym bolshe ne budut soglasovuvat' initsiativy po vnutrennei i vneshnei politike. *Vlast*. Accessed 6 Mar 2022. https://vlast.kz/novosti/48393-s-nazarbaevym-bolse-ne-budut-soglas ovyvat-iniciativy-po-vnutrennej-i-vnesnej-politike.html

Vlast. (2019, April 29). Pyat' sutok aresta dali eshchyo odnomu almatintsu za plakat. *Vlast*. Accessed 6 Mar 2022. https://vlast.kz/novosti/32961-pat-sutok-aresta-dali-ese-odnomu-almatincu-za-plakat.html

Wheeler, G. (1964). *The modern history of soviet Central Asia*. Weidenfield and Nicolson.

White, D. (2015). Political opposition in Russia: The challenges of mobilisation and the political-civil society nexus. *East European Politics, 31*(3), 314–325.

Williamson, S., & Magaloni, B. (2020). Legislatures and policy making in authoritarian regimes. *Comparative Political Studies, 53*(9), 1525–1543.

Witt, M. T. (2011). Exit, voice, loyalty revisited: Contours and implications for public administration in dark times. *Public Integrity, 13*(1), 239–251.

Wright, J. (2008). Do authoritarian institutions constrain? How legislatures affect economic growth and investment. *American Journal of Political Science, 52*(2), 322–343.

Yanovskaya, M., & Kislov, D. (2012, December 16). God posle Zhanaozena. Sudy nespravedlivy, oppozitsiya obezglavlena, repressii usilivayutsya. *Ferghana.ru*. Accessed 25 Jan 2022. https://www.fergananews.com/articles/7571

Yessenova, S. (2010), Borrowed places: Eviction wars and property rights formalization in Kazakhstan. In D. C. Wood (Ed.), *Economic action in theory and practice: Anthropological investigations* (pp. 11–45). Research in Economic Anthropology, Vol. 30. Emerald Group Publishing Limited.

Zaslavskaya, M. B. (1994). *Politicheskie partii i obshchestvennye ob'edineniya Kazakhstana na sovermennom etape razvitiia*. KISI.

Zhandayeva, R., and Zhanmukanova, A. (2022, January 10). Kazakhstan's instability has been building for years. *Foreign Policy*. Accessed online 5 Mar 2022. https://foreignpolicy.com/2022/01/10/kazakhstan-instability-protests-nazarbayev/

Zhani, F. (2007, August 19). Kazakhstan Kontr-evoliotsiia parlamenta, ili Kratkaia istoriia izgnaniia oppozitsii. *Fergana.ru*. Accessed 20 Dec 2021. http://www.ferghana.ru/article.php?id=5295

Zhoyamergen, O. (2019, February 6). Posobiya, zhil'e, otstavka ministra. Mnogodetnye ozvuchili trebovaniya. *Radio Azattyk*. Accessed 3 Mar 2022. https://rus.azattyq.org/a/kazakhstan-astana-mothers-with-many-children/29754282.html

Zhoyamergen, O. (2020, December 1) 'Sl'shashchee gosudarstvo' Tokaeva: skazannoe vs sdelannoe. *Radio Azattyk*. Accessed 5 Mar 2022. https://rus.azattyq.org/a/tokayev-said-vs-done/30999995.html

Ziegler, C. E. (2010). Civil society, political stability, and state power in Central Asia: Cooperation and contestation. *Democratization, 17*(5), 795–825.

Zimanov, S. (2011). *Parlament Kazakhstana v trudnye gody provozglasheniya nezavisimosti*. Alash baspasy.

Index

A
Abilov, Bolat, 35, 76, 78, 81, 82, 85, 87–90, 128, 131
Abish, Samat, 118
Ablyazov, Mukhtar, 35, 76, 78, 81, 82, 85–87, 91, 97, 100, 105, 111, 113, 131
Akikat (Truth), 64
Aktau, 103, 108
Aktobe, 101, 108
AK Zhol (Bright Path), 81, 85–88, 92, 113, 131
Alash Orda, 59
Alash Party, 59, 64
Alga (Forward), 87, 105
Aliyev, Rakhat, 70, 77–82, 91
Alma-Ata Peoples Front, 64
Almaty, 64, 67, 76, 77, 81, 86–90, 99, 101, 102, 110, 111, 113–116
Anti-system opposition, 27
Arab Spring, 31
Arendt, Hannah, 1
Assembly of Peoples of Kazakhstan (APK), 67, 108
Authoritarian resilience, 2, 4, 6
Azat (Freedom), 89
Azerbaijan, 28

B
Baimenov, Alikhan, 81, 82, 85, 88, 90, 131
Bazargali, Medina, 110
Belarus, 28, 116
Blondel, Jean, 21
Brezhnev, Leonid, 60–62
Bureaucratic Authoritarianism, 1

C
Communist Party of Kazakhstan, 60, 66, 68
Corporatism, 2

© The Author(s), under exclusive license to Springer Nature Switzerland AG 2022
R. Isaacs, *Political Opposition in Authoritarianism*, The Theories, Concepts and Practices of Democracy, https://doi.org/10.1007/978-3-031-06536-1

D

Dahl, Robert, 5, 21, 23, 24, 27
Democratic Party of Kazakhstan, 115
Democratic transition, 22
Demokraticheskii Vybor Kazakhstana (Democratic Choice of Kazakhstan, DVK), 6, 76

E

East Germany (GDR), 8, 42
Education, 26, 29, 59
Election protests (2019), 10, 52, 102, 109
Estonia, 8
Exit, 8–14, 35, 36, 41–51, 53, 58, 67, 70, 71, 75, 76, 79, 83, 85, 87, 89, 91–93, 97, 105–107, 115, 119, 130–134
  exit tax, 47, 50

F

Federation of Labour Unions of Kazakhstan, 104, 106

G

Glasnost, 62
Gorbachev, Mikhail, 62, 65

H

Hirschman, Albert, vii, 8–11, 35, 36, 41, 42, 44–46, 115, 130

I

Institutional adaptation, 9–14, 23, 35, 36, 44, 47–53, 57, 65, 66, 75, 76, 83, 85, 86, 89, 90, 93, 102, 105–107, 109, 113, 114, 119, 129, 131, 132

Institutional Revolutionary Party (PRI), 42, 43

K

Kazakh Autonomous Soviet Socialist Republic, The, 58
Kazhegeldin, Akezhan, 35, 76, 77, 79, 80, 83–86, 90, 91, 93, 97, 129
KazMunaiGas, 103–105
Khrushchev, Nikita, 60
Kolbin, Gennady, 63
Korenizatsiia (nativisation), 59
Kosanov, Amirzhan, 84
Kozhakhmetov, Assylbek, 113
Kozlov, Vladimir, 87, 105
Kulibayev, Timur, 105, 106, 118
Kunaev, Dinmukhamed, 60–63
Kyrgyzstan, 99, 104, 133
Kyzylorda, 108

L

Land Protests (2016), 6, 10, 52, 107, 109, 113
Law on Political Parties (1996), 68
Law on Political Parties (2002), 86, 87, 92
Liberal democracy, 24, 25
Linz, Juan, 6, 23
Lobbying, 26, 29, 78
Loyalty, 3, 8–12, 27, 35, 36, 41–44, 46–51, 61, 62, 67, 69–71, 78, 82, 83, 87, 88, 90, 115, 129–131

M

Mamay, Zhanbolat, 115
Mangistau, 103, 105
Masimov, Karim, 116, 118

Mazhilis (legislature), 78, 81, 88, 107, 110, 118
Musayev, Alnur, 79

N
Nagiz AK Zhol (Real Bright Path), 88, 89
National Council of Public Trust, 113, 114
National delimitation, 58
National Security Committee of Kazakhstan (KNB), 79, 84, 88, 116, 118
Nazarbayeva, Dariga, 82
Nazarbayev, Nursultan, 6, 10–13, 23, 29, 31, 35, 43, 52, 57, 62, 65–71, 75–78, 80–82, 84, 85, 87, 88, 90–92, 98–100, 104–106, 108–112, 116, 118, 119, 129, 131, 132
Nevada-Semipalatinsk International Anti-nuclear and Ecological Movement, 63
Nurkadilov, Zamanbek, 76–79, 88
Nur Otan (Light of Fatherland), 84, 88, 90, 118

O
Obshchnatsional'noi sotsial-demokraticheskoi partii (All-National Social Democratic Party [OSDP]), 89, 90, 92
Oralman (returnee), 106
Otan (Fatherland), 78, 81, 84
Oyan, Kazakhstan (Wake up, Kazakhstan), 100, 111, 115, 128, 132

P
Party of Peoples Congress of Kazakhstan, 66

Pavlodar, 63, 108
Perestroika, 62
Peruashev, Azat, 88
Polyarchy, 22, 24
Privatisation, 67, 69, 71

Q
Qandy Qantar (bloody January), 6, 13, 52, 98, 115, 117–119, 129, 132

R
Republican Peoples Party of Kazakhstan (RPNK), 80, 84
Russia, 27, 28, 31, 34, 69, 70, 112, 116

S
Sanctions, 5, 9, 10
Sarsenbayev, Altynbek, 88
Satybaldy, Kairat, 118
Semey, 108
Social Democratic Party of Kazakhstan, 64
Socialist Party of Kazakhstan, 66
Social media, 26, 28, 29, 31, 51, 107, 108, 110, 112, 113
Sokolova, Natalya, 103
Soviet Union (USSR), 2, 57–62, 64, 133
Street protests, 27–29, 31
Suleimenov, Olzhas, 63, 66, 67

T
Taldykorgan, 118
Tokayev, Kassym-Zhomart, 98, 101, 109, 110, 113, 114, 116–119, 132
Tolymbekov, Beibarys, 111

Trade Unions, 27, 30, 51, 97, 100, 103, 104, 106, 128
Tuleshov, Tokhtar, 109
Tulesova, Asya, 111
Tuyakbai, Zharmakhan, 81, 88–90, 92

U
Umbrella Movement, Hong Kong, 31
Union of Peoples Unity of Kazakhstan (SNEK), 66
Uralsk, 108, 111

V
Voice
  collective voice, 46
  horizontal voice, 46
  private voice, 49, 75, 77, 79
  public voice, 12, 45, 47, 48, 50, 51, 75, 76, 81, 83, 85, 92, 98–100, 102, 107, 110–112, 114, 115, 130–132
vertical voice, 49, 50

Z
Zelenogo Fronta (Green Front), 63
Zhakiyanov, Galyman, 76
Zhanaozen protests (2011), 6, 103
Zhandosov, Oraz, 78, 82, 85, 88–90, 113, 131
Zheltokan (December)
  events, 63
  party, 63
Zhovtis, Yevgeni, 117
Zhukeev, Tulegen, 88, 89

GPSR Compliance

The European Union's (EU) General Product Safety Regulation (GPSR) is a set of rules that requires consumer products to be safe and our obligations to ensure this.

If you have any concerns about our products, you can contact us on

ProductSafety@springernature.com

In case Publisher is established outside the EU, the EU authorized representative is:

Springer Nature Customer Service Center GmbH
Europaplatz 3
69115 Heidelberg, Germany

www.ingramcontent.com/pod-product-compliance
Ingram Content Group UK Ltd.
Pitfield, Milton Keynes, MK11 3LW, UK
UKHW021251180426
11946UKWH00004B/80